SEABIRDS
OF THE WORLD

SEABIRDS
OF THE WORLD

Photographs by Eric Hosking   Text by Ronald M Lockley

Facts On File Publications
460 Park Avenue South
New York, N.Y. 10016

To the memory of a brilliant field ornithologist, Sir Julian Huxley FRS, who encouraged and shared with us the study of birds in nature.

SEABIRDS OF THE WORLD

First published in the United Kingdom in 1983 by Croom Helm Ltd., Provident House, Burrell Row, Beckenham, Kent, BR3 1AT.

First published in the United States of America in 1984 by Facts On File, Inc. 460 Park Avenue South, New York, N.Y. 10016

Library of Congress Cataloging in Publication Data
Main entry under title:

Seabirds of the world.

   1. Sea birds. I. Hosking, Eric. II. Lockley, R. M.
(Ronald Mathias), 1903–
QL673.S29 1984   598.4   83-1751
ISBN 0-87196-249-7

Designed by Elgin Press Limited
Printed and bound in Great Britain

Title page A whirling mass of fulmars, Arctic terns, Kittiwakes and Glaucous gulls, at the vast Monaco Glacier in Liefdefjorden, Spitsbergen.

Above Scenes at a breeding colony of the Blue-eyed Cormorant, *P. atriceps*, at Port Lochroy, Antartica.

Overleaf The Black-billed Gull, *L. bulleri* is simply a dark-billed, black-legged offshoot of the Red-billed (Silver) Gull, confined to New Zealand where it nests principally inland by lakes and river beds. It is less of a scrounger on man.

Contents

6 Acknowledgements

8 Introduction

14 CHAPTER 1
The Seabird as an Individual

44 CHAPTER 2
Penguins

66 CHAPTER 3
The Petrels

96 CHAPTER 4
**Cormorants, Gannets,
Boobies and others**

120 CHAPTER 5
Skuas, Gulls and Terns

146 CHAPTER 6
The Auks

158 Index and Bibliography

Acknowledgements

Photographing some of the world's seabirds has given me immense pleasure because it has taken me to every continent in the world and I have made innumerable friends. First and foremost of these is Ronald Lockley and I would like to express my gratitude to him for writing such a splendid text. He is the author of more than 50 books and has a unique way of writing about the most scientific subjects in a lucid, fascinating way which makes you want to read on and on.

Many hours were spent at the stern of the *Lindblad Explorer* photographing the albatrosses, petrels, shearwaters and gulls that followed the ship and I would like to thank the Lindblads for inviting me to go on board. If ever you have an opportunity of going on an expedition on this ship do not miss it – you really do explore and visit places to which no other ship ventures. It was after visiting the Antarctic with Ronald on the *Explorer* that we travelled through New Zealand and were joined by Geoff Moon, who made it possible for me to photograph several of the cormorants, terns and gulls.

While staying in California with Dr and Mrs Ralph Buchsbaum, and later in Washington State with Van and Peggy van Sant, I succeeded in getting pictures of many of the west-coast pelagic species and I am grateful to them for all the many miles they drove me in our search for them.

Our visit to the Galapagos Islands, again with Lindblad, was most productive with its boobies, frigatebirds and those unique gulls, the Lava and the nocturnal Swallow-tailed. I would particularly like to thank the International Council for Bird Preservation for allowing us to stay on the island of Cousin in the Seychelles inhabited by the lovely White Terns, noddies and shearwaters – all so tame I could not fail to get photographs.

It was well away from the sea that I photographed the White-necked Cormorant, the African Darter and the White-winged Black Terns and I am grateful to John Williams, who lived in Kenya for so many years, for helping me to take these and some of the other portraits.

Once again I am delighted to include a few of the photographs taken by the late Niall Rankin, whose negatives are now in our collection. These are of the Wandering Albatross display, the White-chinned and Leach's Petrels and the St Kildan with his catch of fulmars taken many years ago. My daughter, Margaret Woodward, took the photograph of the Manx Shearwater while staying on the Isle of Rhum. Her husband, Jeremy, gallantly stood his ground while a Great Skua mobbed him on the Shetland island of Fetlar, so that I could obtain pictures showing the bird's aggressive nature in its breeding territory. Dr D. P. Wilson kindly gave us permission to use his photo-micrograph of zooplankton. The portrait of the Great Auk was taken in the Icelandic Museum in Reykjavik where the late Dr Finnur Gudmundsson kindly made arrangements for me to take it.

My son, David, has helped me in many ways not least of which has been providing 14 of the photographs that appear in this book and worthy of special mention is his black and white picture of the Sandwich Tern feeding its young, taken when he was only eleven years old.

The layout of a book of this kind is no easy task and I am extremely grateful to Simon Blacker for all the trouble he has taken to make it so attractive. Christopher Helm, my publisher, and his Natural History Editor, Jo Hemmings, have by their enthusiasm and understanding made my task so much easier.

In travelling the world, Dorothy, my wife, has usually been at my side always ready to give me every possible assistance – I cannot thank her enough.

Over the many years it has taken to compile the photographs in this book there has been a host of people who have given me invaluable aid and although they have not been mentioned by name I am nevertheless very indebted to them all.

I hope that this book helps others to enjoy the seabirds of the world and gives them as much pleasure as they have given me.

Eric Hosking

Introduction

The beauty and grace of the flying bird compel admiration and wonder. It is an aesthetic appeal to eye and mind when, for a while, we pause to observe the apparently effortless ease with which birds flap and fly, hover and soar. Seabirds seem especially expert in aerial manoeuvres when we watch them, perhaps because it is usually when we have leisure to stand and stare, as at the seaside or aboard ship. Often, hovering or moving slowly near us in the sea wind, a gull, tern, petrel or albatross appears to return that stare of ours intelligently, its bright eyes momentarily examining us closely. Obviously (we may suppose) this is not for any aesthetic reason, but for some advantage the bird may discover of food, or merely because the displacement of air-flow by the obstacle of the cliff, pier or ship we are watching from gives better lift to sustain its flight; or for both reasons.

We have often tried to analyse this fleeting exchange of visual communication with the passing bird, well aware that it is a highly sentient creature, however much we may consider that it is moved principally by instinct – a somewhat ambiguous word we use to cover up our own ignorance of innate (inherited) behaviour patterns in all animals, including man. For us there remains the continual pleasure and challenge of studying the mind and behaviour of birds, a delight springing from our strong curiosity to learn the why, wherefore and whence of their remarkably diverse lives. For many it is a form of escapism – certainly it has been for us: at times we wish we could exchange our plodding earth-bound existence and take wing ourselves into the clean sky with such ease, even to follow summer across the equator as many migrant birds do, who know no winter in their lives.

Some such thoughts – a mixture of human curiosity and acquisitiveness – led me as a young man to live with, and study, seabirds and other groups, alone at first as a young man on a remote Welsh island of 100 hectares. Skokholm has since become an observatory, the first in Britain, where field studies of island and oceanic birds have continued for more than fifty years. A similar inquisitiveness has inspired Eric Hosking to answer the life-long challenge to photograph the natural lives of seabirds. The present book is the happy result of sharing our experiences in seabird studies in many oceans

around the world. Fortunately we were both encouraged, early in our careers, by two leading ornithologists of their day. First to advise me in my island studies was Harry F. Witherby, known today as the father of both modern museum and field ornithology, founder of the monthly journal *British Birds*, and its ringing scheme, and editor of the first comprehensive *Handbook of British Birds*. Recognising my unique opportunity for studying at Skokholm what was at that time (1928) virtually unknown – the breeding biology of the Manx Shearwater, *Puffinus puffinus*, and Storm Petrel, *Hydrobates pelagicus* – he supplied me with the essential means by which the individual can be identified: numbered leg-rings (or bands as they are more usually called today) from his *British Birds* scheme. This was then still in its

infancy, but has since been developed to its present success and efficiency under the British Trust for Ornithology and the Nature Conservancy. Witherby was a frequent early visitor to my island.

Another friend of both Eric and myself was the veteran biologist W.B. Alexander, who became first Director of the Edward Grey Institute of Field Ornithology at Oxford. I can still see 'W.B.' (as he was affectionately dubbed) diving through an ancient cork lifebuoy from the wreck of the schooner *Alice Williams* which had, fortunately for me, provided material for the repair of the little house soon after I landed to live at Skokholm. It was a feat which mystified us, but W.B. was proud of it, since the measured circumference of his large stomach exceeded by a few inches that of the

interior ring of the buoy! Alexander was a Johnsonian figure, admiring but criticising the studies of seabirds he was so expert in identifying himself, having in 1928 produced his classic *Birds of the Ocean: a Handbook for Voyagers*. This condensed guide to the seabirds of the world, chiefly their distribution, has run into many editions. We recommend it here as still one of the best books to fit the pocket of the traveller who will need to identify oceanic birds from the detailed plumage descriptions Alexander gives.

W.B. Alexander was deeply interested in establishing coastal bird observatories. Together we had the pleasure of joining Edinburgh ornithologists in setting up, in 1934, the second British one on the Isle of May in the Firth of Forth. More such stations have been established at strategic sites

Preceding page The Glaucous Gull, *Larus hyperboreus*. The adult Glaucous has a very pale mantle and the wing-quills are white, as shown in this picture of one following our ship at Spitsbergen. It is a circumpolar breeder, nesting along the whole of the Arctic coast.

Above Herring Gulls *Larus argentatus* taking fish offal thrown overboard from a boat passing Hilbre Island, Cheshire.

around the British Isles, including Jersey, and there are now several abroad which Eric and I have visited, for example in the Galapagos Islands and New Zealand. Such stations have enabled ornithologists to complete monographs and scientific papers on seabirds. We have freely drawn on these in this book, as acknowledged in the bibliography.

There is still much more to be discovered and this is part of the pleasure of bird-watching. According to systematists, who not infrequently dispute over and change the (artificial) specific and subspecific rank, and thereby the scientific names, of living organisms, there are between 270 and 280 species of seabirds, classified in four Orders containing 18 families if we include the ocean-going waders, the phalaropes, and the more estuarine darters.

In this largely pictorial record of the living seabird it has not been possible to describe and illustrate more than a limited number of species of our more personal intimate acquaintance, typical of those families. But in doing so it is our hope that the reader will share with us in actively supporting their protection and conservation, so much needed today in a world where man increasingly destroys or exploits their nesting grounds. In this book we visit many sanctuaries established specially to protect birds on shores which are no longer remote but have become accessible within a few hours by swift modern transport. To see and study and understand something of their beauty and remarkable adaptation to seagoing life is a great privilege, and one which we must preserve for future generations. But many more such nature reserves are needed if we are to save the more endangered species.

Please support your national conservation organisations, and world-wide wildlife protection societies such as the Audubon Society of America, the Royal Society for the Protection of Birds of the British Isles, and the World Wildlife Fund.

Ronald Lockley

The White-necked Cormorant, *Phalacrocorax lucidus*, photographed at a tree roost in Kenya.

CHAPTER 1
The Seabird as an Individual

It may be asked, 'What is a seabird?' A good question, and one which we can only attempt to answer briefly here through a sketch of the origin, evolution and wonderful adaptation of seabirds, on the one hand to ocean wandering, and at the other extreme to a non-migratory, sometimes largely inland, existence: some have even become flightless diving birds. Several in the same family have diverged surprisingly in life-style and distribution. For example the European Cormorant, *Phalacrocorax carbo*, makes a migration of several hundred miles from its nesting site and is distributed almost world-wide between the sub-Arctic and sub-Antarctic latitudes; but the Galapagos Cormorant, *Nannopterum harrisi*, is so completely stay-at-home that its wings have become atrophied and can no longer lift it in flight.

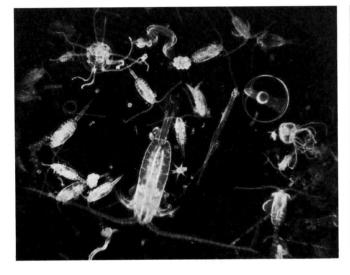

Above Zooplankton of the marine food chain (×25 approx).

Right The Pelagic Cormorant, *Phalacrocorax pelagicus*, associates with the larger more abundant Brandt's Cormorant, *P. penicillatus*, in off-duty roosting, preening and sunning along the Californian shore at Monterey. Both are black, but note the smaller head and bill of the Pelagic species, which also develops a white flank patch in the breeding season.

Overleaf Lesser Black-backed Gulls, *Larus fuscus*, are migratory, feeding much in coastal waters and following ships (as here, off the Norwegian shore). It breeds on all coasts of north-west Europe, and Iceland, ranging in winter to the Mediterranean, North Africa and the Atlantic isles. It prefers to nest colonially where vegetative cover grows to shelter its chicks, enabling them to hide when the colony is disturbed by prowling mammals, including man.

Even in such truly oceanic species as the petrels, including albatrosses, shearwaters and storm petrels, we find within the same genus that one species is a pelagic transequatorial migrant, another is a partial migrant roaming perhaps 500 kilometres from home, while a third is more or less sedentary within sight of the breeding island or cliffs. Yet these tube-nosed birds, as ornithologists call them collectively, rarely alight on the land except when breeding. Watching their perfect control of long-duration flight one has the impression that, if only they could, some would nest on the surface of the sea. An impossibility of course, but such a fleeting thought has occurred to us when admiring the graceful flight of a tropicbird or bos'n bird above the weed-strewn Sargasso Sea, at least a thousand kilometres from the nearest land.

The Food Chain of the Sea

The main reason for the maintenance activity which ensures the survival of all living creatures is perfectly basic and simple: in one word, food. We shall try to show, as we describe the lives typical of the main family groups, how each seabird has developed to fill one of the different ecological niches of food and territory of the marine habitat just as successfully as terrestrial birds share those of the land. It may seem strange, but although there are fewer species in total, numerically there are more individual seabirds than land birds in the world. We need to remember that about three-quarters of the earth's surface is covered by salt water; and that this is just as rich as the land in food; sometimes richer.

The Seabird as an Individual

Seabirds are able to exploit salt water in depth, from the tidal and estuarine perimeter of tropical and polar lands, to the wide open ocean. Some obtain their food at or just above the surface, some by diving to varied depths below – and of these divers some 'fly' under water with flippers or half-open wings, while others use only the webbed feet to propel their streamlined bodies in pursuit of their selected aquatic prey.

More than half the seabird species subsist, as might be expected, on vertebrate fish as their main food. The larger birds take the larger fish, up to the limit of their swallowing capacity – often competing with man for commercially marketable species, as anyone may see from the activity around trawlers and other seafishing vessels hauling their gear. Gulls, gannets, cormorants and many species of petrel flock to the ship's side to devour escaping fish and the offal thrown overboard during gutting operations. However, the smaller species, such as some auks, the prions and storm petrels, and most of the penguins (heaviest of seabirds), like the giant baleen whales live much, and some altogether, on small invertebrate organisms known as zooplankton or krill. This is really a considerable advantage, as zooplankton is near the base of the seafood chain, found universally in all seas, and always available to a diving species. It consists of tiny animals such as shrimps, crabs and other crustaceans, squid, jellyfish, sea worms and many other free-swimming creatures, in both larval and adult forms. These animals browse largely on the phytoplankton – the microscopic plants, including algae, which are the lowest strata of the food chain and the most abundant and prolific, multiplying by cell division as they drift through the sea. They obtain energy as land plants do, by photosynthesis (sunlight trapped by their chlorophyll and used to build living tissue from a combination of the elements of air and water).

As we shall note presently, the long hours of sunlight of the polar summer favour rapid photosynthesis, while the usually violent winds and strong currents of Arctic and Antarctic latitudes cause an upwelling of water which lifts and mixes the mineral salts which in the calm tropics sink to the bottom of the windless oceans. From the living components of the food chain – from the plankton up to the large fishes, birds,

Left At the nest the Arctic Tern, *Sterna paradisaea*, aggressively swoops at intruding birds or mammals. We have been repeatedly struck on the head by the dagger-sharp bill. It is essential to wear a thick cap when trespassing in an Arctic Tern colony; without one you may suffer a bloody crown.

Above *Larus novaehollandiae* is the name of the red-billed, red-legged gull of New Zealand, better known as the Silver Gull in Australia and South Africa, and smallest of the few gulls nesting south of the Tropic of Capricorn. Abundant as a scavenger in New Zealand.

Left The beautiful Bridled or Brown-winged Tern, *Sterna anaethetus*, another numerous Seychelles inhabitant, and widespread on many islands of all tropical oceans, flies with ethereal grace on its long narrow wings and forked tail.

cetaceans and seals – there is a constant rain of organic matter in the form of faeces and dead bodies. Much of this waste is devoured and later excreted by free-moving crustaceans and other scavengers of the sea floor. Thus the upswirling waters of the polar regions, although only a few degrees above freezing, are richer in this basic recycled food than the warm motionless 'doldrum' seas of the equatorial belt. Further, the cold water slows down growth and maturity of the zooplankton so that many of these tiny animals live comparatively much longer than their tropical representatives, and pass the winter in larval form – in effect, cold-stored for the return of the whales, penguins and other sea life in the polar spring.

The Senses

Vision. Seabirds need, and have, acute vision, but adapted to the individual's specific way of life. At sea the light is so bright that most species have rather small eyes placed laterally at either side of the head, giving a wide field of view of about 340°. The eye is protected by a nictitating membrane, a thin third lid which is drawn across the eye from the nasal side, cleaning it with the tears of the lachrymal gland. It also has a protective function, used automatically to shield the eye against contact with harmful objects, as when fighting, feeding young, or digging a burrow. Some diving birds (including ducks, auks and divers, which feed under the water) have a clear central lens-like panel in the skin of the nictitating membrane – a kind of retractable contact lens – the better to see their prey. Like the owls, some dusk- and night-feeding birds such as the skimmers and the Swallow-tailed Gull, *Creagrus furcatus*, have large eyes to gather more light. Birds see colours clearly, otherwise there would be no meaning to their bright plumage.

Generally the bird eye has better acuity than that of man, but is much less mobile in its socket. Instead, the neck is far more flexible, and in most species can be turned through 380° to scan the widest field without turning the body. The position of the eyes of most seabirds, in the side of the head, gives monocular vision: in theory each eye feeds a separate image to the brain. In practice, however, seabird eyes can effectively concentrate on any near object in which the bird is interested, as when picking up nesting material, or food, or preening its mate's neck. Gannets and boobies have more

The Common or Brown Noddy, *Anous stolidus*, shares the tropical zones of all three oceans with the Lesser Noddy, but rarely travels far out of sight of land. In contrast with the latter it swims readily, though normally fishing by plunge-diving.

Left The robust and striking Large-billed Tern, *Phaetusa simplex*, is confined to the tropical rivers of South America. Here photographed on the shores of the Amazon.

Right Roseate Tern, *Sterna dougallii*, at nest on Farne Islands.

frontally placed eyes which give binocular vision, assisting the birds to spot fish as they hover and plunge-dive.

Hearing. This sense is as acute as in any animal which is able to recognise the individual voice of its mate, offspring, or the strange note of an antagonist of the same species. There is no evidence that seabirds hear ultrasounds as high as those uttered by bats, or mice, though probably owls are able to. Seabirds' ears are small and hidden by the head feathers, but are adequate for their main purpose, to hear in communication with other birds around them.

Smell. In general it is thought that birds have a poor sense of smell. The olfactory lobe in the bird brain is small, although the nasal passages are well developed as in man, and serve the same purpose of cleaning and moistening the air before it reaches the lungs. In those species which dive much the nostrils are narrow slits in the sides of the upper mandible; in the penguins, cormorants and gannets they are externally closed and breathing is effected through the corner of the mouth. It has been proved however that the tube-nosed seabirds, the petrel family, which have large nostrils, do have a keen sense of smell and can detect, from a distance of several kilometres before they can see it, fatty or oily food floating behind whaling and other ships.

Taste. In birds, which swallow food without mastication since they have no teeth, a sense of taste seems almost lacking. Birds have less than 100 taste buds in the mouth, whereas man has about 9,000. But the tongues of many seabirds, and sometimes also the roof of the mouth, are furnished with short incurving spines or papillae which assist in holding fish and planktonic food, especially when gathering a quantity with which to feed young at the nest (penguins, puffins).

Water needs. It is interesting that seabirds which have no opportunity to drink fresh water are seen to drink sea water freely. To avoid overloading the kidneys and renal system with salt, the excess sodium is conveyed through the blood stream to the nasal glands, where it is disposed of by discharge in the form of a 'nose-drip'.

Feather Care

Seabirds need to maintain their normal body temperature at around 40°C, which is a few degrees above that of man. They do this by constant feather care to avoid chilling or overheating, and to keep the plumage in perfect condition for flying or swimming. Hours are spent daily in preening the body and wing feathers, using the beak or the back of the head as a brush to pick up the oil from the special gland above the tail, and for 'lubricating' the plumage. This action, no doubt the result of a natural itchiness, ensures the smooth interlocking or 'zipping together' of the barbules along each shaft of a feather with its neighbour, each feather overlapping like the tiles on a roof and covered with a film of preen oil to make the whole waterproof. This conserves a cushion of warm air against the skin from which body heat emanates.

After feeding, seabirds meticulously wash themselves in the nearest water, preferably fresh water, but also freely in salt water. It is remarkable to watch gulls, terns, skuas, seaducks and many petrels bathing in even the coldest water, barely above freezing, with a dipping, scooping movement of the head and neck – tossing water backwards over the body so that it penetrates to the down-covered skin beneath the feathers, which are deliberately opened for that purpose by contraction of the skin-muscles. Like scratching and yawning in man, these preening actions are often infectious and will ripple through a flock at rest. (Birds also yawn a lot.) But it will be noted that however wet the bathing bird gets, as soon as it rises up in flight, or walks ashore and shakes its whole body, as a dog does on leaving the water, the last drops at once roll off the oily exterior. During intensive preening, any feather scale, loose down or body parasites gathered in the searching beak are invariably swallowed; it is believed that the weathered preen oil also ingested at that moment may be of medicinal benefit, since after long irradiation in sunlight it is rich in vitamin D.

Radiation from sunlight at the open nest on warm days often produces local temperatures far above comfortable

The Seabird as an Individual

The Little Shag, as *Phalacrocorax melanoleucus* is rather confusingly called in New Zealand, is a variable species of black-footed freshwater cormorant identical with the so-called White-throated (or Little Pied) Shag of Australia. This group, at rest at Lake Taupo, central North Island, New Zealand, happen to be the dark phase, but there is a white-throated form, and a pied phase almost identical with the Pied *P. varius*, distinguished by its much smaller size – 56 cm compared with 81 cm long in the larger bird. Also look for the small, shorter bill in *P. melanoleucus*. It is largely an inland lake breeder, sharing at times the same tree with other black-footed shags.

body heat. In that case, as birds are unable to cool their bodies by perspiring, they do so by opening the mouth and 'panting' – inducing a flow of air to and from the lungs by rapid oscillation of the throat. At the same time the wings (flippers in the penguins) are half-opened. To protect the young from fierce noonday heat during their early down stage at the nest, parent cormorants, boobies and frigatebirds will shade them with widely spread wings. This action seems to be less instinctive than intelligent. It has survival value, and could have been learned by the adult while still a tender hatchling. In opening its own wings the parent is at the same time helping to cool its own body, though basically the manoeuvre springs from the bird's strong instinct to brood and protect its progeny.

All birds are troubled by external parasites, transmitted to the young during brooding at the nest. Lice, which in birds fortunately do not suck blood as mammal lice do, live on feather scale and debris; and most birds have lice specific to their species or genus. Lice live warmly and permanently attached to the feathers, and there are sometimes different species inhabiting different areas of the plumage. One species even burrows into the hollow shafts of the larger feathers, where it is safe from preening – but not from the danger of being cast out into the cold when the feather is moulted. Most birds also carry their specific blood-sucking flea. The adult bird flea lives, mates and feeds permanently on the body of a healthy bird. Perfectly adapted for survival, the female is most active in laying her eggs while the bird host is brooding at the nest. The eggs tumble into the bottom of the warm nest where they hatch into larvae and feed on decaying matter containing protein, in particular the droppings of adult fleas, which contain residues of undigested blood. They then pupate, and under continuing warmth soon emerge as perfect fleas to infest the young bird. The last generation of the season may hibernate in egg or larval form over the winter, to be warmed into life by the adult bird returning to the nest again. Human fleas follow much the same cycle; it is well known that the movement and warmth of man, returning to a flea-infested house, triggers flea larvae to hatch and leap towards a mammalian source of heat.

We must mention an even more serious blood-sucking parasite, though it is strictly short-term and seasonal. Various species of tick attach themselves to seabirds, espe-

Left The handsome dusky-plumaged Heermann's Gull, *Larus heermanni*, photographed at Monterey Bay, California, is resident along the Pacific coast from Vancouver to Southern Mexico.

Right Little Terns, *Sterna albifrons* – courtship feeding: male giving a sand eel to his mate.

Below right Sabine's Gull, *Larus sabini*, beside nest, Alaska.

cially in long-established nesting sites. We have found albatrosses, Razorbills, guillemots, gulls and puffins badly infested with large *Ixodes* ticks which can measure 5mm in girth when engorged with blood. They are almost impossible to remove, so deeply are the tick's proboscis and its recurved spines embedded. However, after each engorgement the tick drops off, to hide in the ground while moulting into a larger skin before emerging to seek its next meal; or else it dies after mating and laying its eggs in the debris, preferably of the bird colony. We have been glad to realise that as soon as an engorged tick drops off a seabird at sea, it must perish by drowning!

Water birds and mammals (seal, whale, dolphin, walrus) are born without internal parasites, but soon acquire them in feeding operations. The zooplankton of the basic salt and fresh water food chain supports numerous nematode and other worms which, in free-swimming form as larvae, or adult or egg, are eaten by fish. Seabirds which eat infested fish act as secondary or final host, usually without serious deterioration of their health. Often a large ball of writhing mature worms will be found in a seabird's stomach; in this congenial medium of the avian intestinal secretions the adult worms are able to resist being digested; they mate, and their eggs and exhausted bodies are voided – to be recycled as described.

The Seabird Brain

We recognise that birds are highly sentient beings, as we are, and although some scientists may scorn what is called anthropomorphism – endowing animals with human-like thoughts and personalities – it is natural that we try to interpret some of their seemingly logical behaviour in the light of our own behaviour and experience. For we are motivated by the same main drives: our inherited, automatic reaction in a given situation, and the conscious learning we derive from experience and observation. Both spring from our physical needs for survival. One difference is that the brain of the bird develops so much faster than ours. In the short span of a few weeks or months, while the human child is a babe at the breast, the average bird develops from the egg to full growth and independence as an adult. We shall describe this surprising precociousness as it varies in the species and families of seabirds; but it will be useful here to summarise briefly the main survival activities common to almost all birds under what has been called the 'three Ms': maintenance (food gathering, avoidance of enemies, sleep); mating (sexual and reproductive activity); and moulting (annual renewal of weatherproof plumage which all birds must undergo – a period of strain and metabolic reorganisation).

Social and Sexual Behaviour

With certain exceptions which help to prove the rule, it is a fact that where, as in almost all seabirds, adult female and male are externally alike in size, plumage, colour and markings, the species is monogamous, and usually a pair will remain faithful to each other as long as both shall live. This faithfulness is the result – as it often is in man – of establishing a partnership at the breeding site, and successfully raising progeny together. Having achieved this union for the first season, the pair will return to the well-remembered site at the start of each subsequent breeding season, even if they spend the intervening period food-seeking apart, as most migratory seabirds do. The pair-bond

Above Black Tern, *Chlidonias niger*, alighting at nest.

Right Adult Dolphin or Magellan Gull, *Gabianus scoresbyi*, a handsome medium-size gull nesting on islets at the extremity of South America. In the Falklands this bird approached us in expectation of food scraps. It is resident as far north as the Valdez Peninsula.

is renewed and maintained at the nest in several stereotyped ways, but principally by individual voice recognition. This of course is essential if they meet at the nest-site only by night, as many of the smaller petrel species do. Love, for these birds, is a voice and a presence in burrow darkness.

The older experienced breeders are the first to return after the winter, and establish or re-establish their claims to nesting territory. The mature male appears first; clearly he must be ready to mate early in the breeding cycle, as soon as his partner begins ovulating. The male announces his presence at the site by calling loudly, and in a diurnal species by displaying at any other bird approaching or passing near, usually with exaggerated movements of the head, bowing and wing-waving, in a pattern which is specific and mono-

tonously repetitive. Such display in birds is a mixture of instinct and learning. Its origin can be traced to the survival movements of the new-born chick. As soon as it hatches from the egg, and often before, it utters peeping sounds of increasing discomfort as it struggles to emerge from the shell. The parent responds with low complacent noises and comfort movements, at intervals tenderly examining and touching with its bill the emerging or emerged chick, coaxing it towards the warmth of the unfeathered skin of the brood-patch under the breast (in the gannet, booby and cormorant which have no bare brood spot, the webbed feet are the warming agent). The parent now sits more lightly to avoid crushing the chick.

Voice recognition is thus established early between parent

and child, even before the chick opens its eyes and sees its parent for the first time. The thin membranous lids which protect the growing eyes before hatching time remain closed by mucus for some time, up to a week in some hole-nesting birds where sight is not immediately important. In burrow darkness and on dark nights in the open it is essential for the parent to establish voice recognition, as until it does it will not recognise the chick if it happens to wander or be displaced from the birthplace. Experiments with diurnal gulls and penguins, and nocturnal petrels and shearwaters, have proved this – and also that if the egg happens to be so displaced (say by a short distance of one metre), these birds will usually ignore it. As a substitute a 'broody' seabird will often accept a golf ball, a tin box, a bottle, even a snowball or

your camera, if it is about the same size or not much larger than its natural egg. Such experiments of course are quite artificial. Normally the brooding bird does not lose its egg or chick. It retains possession, guarding the home fiercely from natural predators or territorial competitors. The new-born is continuously brooded until voice recognition is firmly established. So firmly indeed that should a chick of the same species stray into or near the home of another, it will be driven away as soon as it proves by its different voice that it is a stranger. If it persists (as some 'lost' chicks may) it will be mauled, perhaps even killed, by the hostile adults.

The young bird learns to associate the voice and presence of its parents with the satisfaction of its hunger, and with protection and warmth. Touching and gaping of the bill

during infant feeding remains as part of the adult courtship in all seabirds. In several species (gulls and terns) the male brings food to the female when courting her; she begs for it exactly as the growing chick does, with the same supplicatory opened mouth, quivering wings and plaintive cries. Courtship feeding in gulls has become so ritualised that it serves two important functions. The female partner, with eggs beginning to develop, is substantially nourished by the large portions which the male regurgitates and she plucks from his mouth. At this pre-egg-laying stage, when her hunger is temporarily satisfied, she crouches down as an invitation to copulation. Compare this visual display, which you may witness in any gull colony, with the partnership in the dark hidden burrow of many small petrels, and some

Below Another contrast between related *Larus* gulls. Although larger than the Kelp Gull, the Pacific Gull, *Larus pacificus*, with its massive bill and sub-terminal black tail-band, seems to be retreating since the aggressive Kelp Gull began colonising the coast haunts of *L. pacificus* in Australia in 1958.

Overleaf The Sooty Tern, *Sterna fuscata*, breeds in large gatherings on many tropical islands of the Indian, Pacific and Atlantic Oceans. An estimated 700,000 nest on Bird Island (this picture) in the Seychelles. A great wanderer on tireless wings and long forked tail, travelling hundreds of kilometres away from land in search of fish, it rarely alights on the sea as it snatches food at the surface. Only one egg is laid.

The Seabird as an Individual

auks. There is no courtship feeding; food is brought only to feed the nestling, which in many species never sees its parents clearly, if at all.

The young bird is quick to learn from parental example in species nesting in the open, exposed to the hazards of weather and diurnal predators. It has to learn not only the pleasures of parental protection, but also, if it is to survive, to react correctly to the dangers associated with the warning cries and other signals they give. Depending on its age and species it responds by crouching still, by fleeing, or by stabbing at the unwelcome visitor, copying the adult actions. But there are many hours when, with hunger and sleep temporarily satisfied, and no unwelcome visitors around, the observer is amused to find the family behaving playfully, like a human household. Parents fondly preen and nibble the child's growing down and feathers, the child caresses the adult in the same fashion, but probably more out of growing curiosity. The chick will pick up a stick or other part of the nest-material, and push it about. It will spot an insect crawling near, and crane its head to get a closer view – maybe even take a stab at it, and, more rarely, swallow it. What is happening in neighbouring nests is, of course, of great interest, but becomes boring quickly enough.

The youngster is receiving impressions of its surroundings which it will store in its brain for the rest of its life, enabling it to return here in due course as a hopeful homeseeker, remembering childhood's happy days. However, before – but sometimes after – fledging it must learn the painful lesson that its parents are growing indifferent, and may ultimately become hostile, to its food-begging advances. They are entering the difficult period of the post-breeding moult. At this age the fledgling is usually fat with recent good feeding, and well able to stand a long fast. But in its inexperience it may approach an unrelated adult, and be viciously attacked. There are many dangers, and the greatest mortality occurs during the first year of the seabird's life, from predators, weather, and starvation. With the family bond broken the adolescent must learn what is known as 'safety distance' – generally at least one body-length – to be out of close striking distance of the next bird. This is the beginning of ter-

ritoriality, not unfamiliar to the young bird of a sociable species, and observed and learned from the warning and threat display of its parents maintaining nesting space in competition with neighbouring pairs, as well as from the alarm or angry cries of the adults pursuing would-be predators approaching their territory.

Adolescence

The young bird has by now learned the threat display of its species – generally a lowering of the head, bill open and pointed at the would-be trespasser, wings partly open, giving an effect of making the bird appear larger than normal. Threat display is more economical, less wasteful of energy, than fighting. It is part of the survival kit of the adolescent and essential if it is to secure a viable place in the flock, for at first it will have a very low status in the hierarchy or peck-order of the winter gatherings during food and roosting activities. Older birds will force it to retreat by more vigorous threat display in competition for tit-bits of food and the more desirable roosting sites.

During the breeding season the adults are normally away from the wintering area; but in many species the juveniles born in the previous season remain there together if the food is attractive. As we note later in the book, in some species maturity is not reached for several years (up to ten in the largest albatrosses), which in round figures means that in the majority of seabirds at any given time there are as many immature or non-breeding individuals as there are es-tablished breeders. In the non-breeding group the individual advances in status, we may suppose, with growing ex-perience of how to survive, as it becomes a senior member of the young flock. Dominance is built up by typical display, both intraspecifically and interspecifically; that is, as we have seen in seabird feeding associations at sea, between in-dividuals of the same species and between those of different species, competing for fish offal released from trawls being hauled. In the scramble for this prized food, large petrels, shearwaters, skuas and gulls jostle each other, the safety-distance rule momentarily ignored, but quickly observed

again as soon as the last morsel has been devoured.

When at last the young seabird is sexually stimulated to make its first return to the nesting site, it usually does so at or near where it was hatched. Banding studies have proved this. Like man, the bird clearly remembers the site which it must associate with its pleasurable early home life: it has hardly any experience of any other place on land if it is an ocean-going petrel, gannet, tropicbird or frigatebird. However, in order to mate it must overcome the barrier of safety distance. This may take so long that successful breeding may be delayed for one or more years. Usually the sexually mature, but never-mated, young bird arrives long after the ex-perienced breeders are established in their territories. In a successful and expanding colony all the best sites will already

Right The very handsome dark Inca Tern, *Larosterna inca*, with its heavy scarlet bill and white handlebar 'moustachio' markings, is confined to the Inca coast of Peru and northern Chile. Because of its striking appearance it has been collected to exhibit in captivity. We have to admit we saw this pair in a zoo in Germany!

Overleaf Bonaparte's Gull, *Larus philadelphia*, is the temperate North American counterpart of the European Black-headed Gull *L. ridibundus*. It has yellow, not red, legs.

be occupied and the first-timer will have to be satisfied with a less desirable spot. Here it will display – in the words of the old song 'doing what comes naturally', which is all it knows by instinct and learning. It will hear and copy the display of the nesting adults in what has been called appetitive behaviour; and if this exhibition attracts an unattached female, the process of breaking down safety distance begins. In gulls, the young male seems to have to discover if the newcomer is female, and when she approaches both utter warning cries and assume aggressive postures. They are outwardly so alike to the human eye that one can well imagine that the young female is also testing the sex of the gull advertising on site. The situation may be further complicated by the arrival of a third sexually interested bird. In gulls, gannets and most

seabirds we have watched, the female indicates her acceptance of a male, and her willingness to mate, by turning aside her head, with its conspicuous colours or markings and its threatening bill. Body contact is made, and mating soon follows. Late in the season copulation may not occur, or if it does, no egg may be laid. But the young pair have become sweethearts, in effect, and plighted their troth at a trysting place to which they will return next year, earlier and more mature. However, where an established breeding bird in possession of a nest-site has lost a mate, he or she will accept a new partner from the reservoir of unmated birds.

We are thus back to where this account of the seabird as an individual began, with the establishment of the pair-bond by voice recognition. A few sedentary birds, notably the larger

Dark phase Arctic Skua, *Stercorarius parasiticus*; a pair at their nest in the Shetlands, feeding their young.

gulls, keep together throughout the year once they have mated; but the majority do not. These renew the pair-bond when the male returns to claim the familiar nest-site, where, if she has survived the winter, his mate will shortly join him. When they meet again after the long separation, the same ritual display takes place; they begin with threat actions, ready to attack until voice recognition is fully established. Display serves to stimulate, and is really a mixture of self-advertisement, fear of attack, and the drive to mate. Even after a short parting, as when one bird has been away feeding for a while, it is greeted with this mixture of hostility and welcome by its mate at home.

If we care to reflect on the nature of display in seabirds, where the sexes are externally so alike, we may see its counterpart in our own behaviour, equally perhaps a mixture of instinct and learning from experience. At the approach of another person we are cautious, even fearful and innately hostile; we utter sharp interrogatory calls ('Who's there?') and subconsciously keep safety distance. But recognising the voice of a harmless acquaintance or a loved one, we respond with a different, quieter tone of voice, and permit body contact: safety distance is no longer essential.

Between mated seabirds (as in most humans) there is also so-called ecstatic behaviour, a ritualised form of the typical greeting display. In some species it lasts throughout, and even after, the long period of mating, incubation and rearing of the family. When together at the nest, the mated pair at intervals indulge in gentler variations of the normal threat-appeasement display, more complacent noises, and frequent mutual preening of each other's head and neck – an eye-level affair technically known as allo-preening. Such continued display serves to heighten the emotional bond and maintain their mutual interest in sharing the domestic duties of rearing their replacement. The mated pair unite to defend the home against intruders and predators by increased threat display and louder cries; or if one partner is temporarily alone at the nest, it will do so. In colonies where the nests are close together, with only narrow safety distances between nests (gannets, penguins, gulls, terns), threat display is almost continuous, but highly ritualised in order to avoid serious fighting between next-door neighbours.

The Seabird as an Individual

There is a reason for everything in nature, if we can discover it. The mass stimulation of crowded seabird colonies leads to close synchronisation of mating and egg-laying, resulting in a less protracted breeding season, and consequently better rearing success. Add to this the fact that large colonies have a relatively smaller perimeter exposed to natural predators, which are the more easily driven off by the massed assembly of breeding seabirds. Conditions are different in those seabirds which incubate their eggs and rear their offspring underground. But although the mated pair rarely see each other in the clear light of day, they call, meet and mate at night in or near the entrance to the burrow, and there display mutually, even to allo-preening (which we

have observed in shearwaters). As we have said, the pair maintain the love-bond by faithful return to the well-remembered site – and by voice-recognition of the loved one in the darkness of burrow and night.

What happens when the sexually mature 'pre-breeder' returns to the colony in search of a home and mate for the first time, but finds no place in which it can begin courting without being driven away by established pairs? From the evidence of banding many thousands of young birds, it is clear that it is these first-time home-seekers which found new colonies, generally at new sites near to, but occasionally far from, the place where they were born. They are the entrepreneurs, and if they succeed in establishing a colony

on some remote island or cliff or shore far from the original centre of population of their species, they form the nucleus from which may arise, through geographic isolation, adaptation to the new environment, and through advantageous mutation of the closed gene-bank, new subspecies and ultimately new species. We deal briefly with this evolution in our next chapter.

This Elegant Tern, *Thalasseus elegans*, was photographed as it was bathing in a river in Lower California. A sedentary species, it migrates occasionally as far as Chile.

CHAPTER 2
Penguins

The dramatis personae of our seabird saga can begin appropriately with one of the most specialised and oldest families, the penguins. Palaeontologists tell us that penguins originated at least 60 million years ago, when birds began to proliferate from the reptilian prototype *Archaeopteryx* of the Dinosaur (early Mesozoic) Era, 150 million years BP (Before Present).

Between 60 and 30 million years BP, giant penguins and the primitive ancestors of pelicans, cormorants, darters, divers, rails and other water birds appeared on seas and shores which, in extent and shape and place, were very different from those of the present. The comparatively new science of tectonics (the study of the movements of the vast plates of the earth's crust) has shown that about 200 million years ago there was just one huge continent. The present location of New York was close to the equator; 'India', 'Australia' and 'Antarctica' formed the southern part of the supercontinent; and what is now Japan was far to the north, near the Arctic Circle. Studies of fossil distributions, palaeomagnetism, and geological evidence of ancient climates reveal the subsequent break-up and dispersal of the land areas. About 135 million years ago South America and Africa were drifting apart in the south, while in the north the separation of North America and Europe gave birth to the North Atlantic – one of the youngest oceans and one which seabirds were late in colonising. It was in the much larger and older Pacific Ocean and its southern connections with the Indian Ocean that most of the seabird families developed. In the last few million years the present familiar shapes of the oceans and continents appeared. North and South America were finally joined by a narrow land bridge – the Isthmus of Panama – separating the expanding Atlantic Ocean from the now contracting, but still immense, Pacific, and thus isolating their more sedentary sea-life species, allowing the development of new species and subspecies in each ocean.

The relatively slow movements of the land masses above sea-level are still continuing. New Zealand is being pulled apart at the rate of about 3mm a year on a drift towards the equator, while the British Isles are rising in the west and sinking in the east at about the same rate. But these slow movements, occurring over many millions of years, have been complicated by relatively recent climatic changes. During the several periods of the Ice Ages over the last half-million years, the build-up of the earth's water in the form of immense ice-caps covering the land mass of Antarctica, Greenland and the sub-Arctic lands has caused a considerable lowering of ocean levels. There were warmer intervals when this ice cover retreated and the oceans rose correspondingly, but during the height of the most recent glaciation, which ended about 12,000 BP, sea-level fell as much as 100 metres.

Innumerable land animals and plants died out in polar and sub-polar lands, but fewer sea creatures were exterminated by the cold centuries. It was an advantage to be oceanic at

this period; to be able to fly or swim away from the frozen extremes towards the warmth of equatorial latitudes. It is reasonably supposed that the several recent Ice Ages encouraged the natural migratory habits which birds, whales, fish and other mobile creatures already practised during their pre-glacial existence. For whether the earth was young or old, summer and winter existed through all ages. Those species which followed the sun to the long summer daylight of polar latitudes, for the sake of the large yield of the reawakened food chain, must have acquired this habit of north-south migration, retreating from the onset of the four-months winter night. But, as we shall see, one penguin – the surviving giant of those prehistoric, pre-glacial centuries – refused to budge, and each winter continues to face the

Thousands of Rockhopper Penguins, *Eudyptes chrysocome*, nest in the Falkland Islands, crowding gregariously. They look so alike to man, yet each recognises its mate by voice and returns faithfully each season to the well-remembered nest site to meet the same partner. Although two eggs are laid, only the second (larger) one is incubated, suggesting the species is evolving to become a single-egg layer, like most penguins.

Left At Paradise Bay, Antarctic Peninsula, Gentoo Penguins, *Pygoscelis papua*, like to nest in rather less crowded conditions, spaced more apart. The central pair may be newcomers, non-breeders discussing a possible partnership for next season, and meanwhile looking around for a suitable rendezvous.

Overleaf Even in summer snow may fall on Torgersen Island, Antarctic Peninsula, where these Adelie Penguins, *P. adeliae*, early build their nests of little stones. In the background lurks a Yellow-billed Sheathbill, *Chionis alba*, an opportunistic scavenger of food dropped by penguins (even impudently snatched from the adult bill while the chick is being fed), carcasses and digested matter in faeces.

coldest temperatures in the world in the most dramatic life-style of any living bird.

Clearly the penguins evolved from flying ancestors to become specialised swimming and diving machines; the embryo penguin sprouts wing-quills but loses them before hatching. The modified wings can no longer be folded, but are used as oars to propel the lozenge-shaped body under water. At high speed (maximum about 16kph) the neck is withdrawn into the shoulders and the small webbed feet are flattened against the stumpy tail to reduce water resistance. Like porpoises, penguins are able to leap clear of the surface, and will do so when migrating or when pursued by such predators as seals and killer whales, but also apparently out of sheer *joie de vivre*. They are well cushioned against the cold, wearing a thick 'vest' of oily down beneath the dense short feathers which sprout over every part of the skin (not in separate feather tracts as in other birds). In addition, they accumulate a thick layer of subcutaneous fat to tide them over periods of fasting when breeding and moulting.

On land, penguins progress laboriously with a comical swaying waddle, flippers half-extended to maintain balance. Rockhopper Penguins, *Eudyptes chrysocome*, are so called because they prefer to hop, often up steep slopes, to reach their nursery which is usually on broken rocky terrain. At rest in their large colonies they mostly stand upright on their small feet, the short stiff tail-feathers useful as props to prevent the birds toppling backwards. When sleeping they may sink forward onto the breast. The breast-down position is also favoured for quick tobogganing progress downhill over snow and ice, shoving the heavy body with flippers and feet on less steep grades.

Penguins delight us by their tameness and almost human social behaviour when we visit their rookeries. But they are tame and able to exist only because hitherto man has been a rare visitor to their remote colonies. On the more frequented coasts of South America and some sub-Antarctic islands, enormous concentrations of breeding penguins were virtually exterminated by crews put ashore from whaling and sealing ships during the nineteenth century, and for some time later. The feathered skins and the oil obtained by boiling their bodies in 'digester vats' became marketable when the skins and oil from the seals inhabiting these shores were

The Little, Blue or Fairy Penguin, *Eudyptula minor*, is the world's smallest – barely 40cm from bill to tail-tip. Confined to New Zealand and the southern coast of Australia. On Phillip Island, near Melbourne, visitors are organised to watch from the sidelines the nocturnal return from the sea of the adult penguins, as they waddle ashore in groups and proceed to nesting burrows inland which are protected from curious tourists by a fence. The scene is floodlit, but the penguins, normally very shy at sea, have long accepted this blaze of publicity. The urgency of family affairs is comically evident in their haste to get home, where they conduct ear-splitting conversations in the darkness underground.

exhausted. Eric and I saw the rusting relics of this cruel practice when we visited Macquarie Island in the *Lindblad Explorer* in 1980. As many as 150,000 Royal, *Eudyptes schlegeli*, King, *Aptenodytes patagonicus*, Gentoo, *Pygoscelis papua*, and other penguins were annually thrown into these digesters, until the Tasmanian Government, on the objection of Sir Douglas Mawson (leading to an outcry in the world press), cancelled the 'sealing' licence in 1920. We were pleased to find that, with Macquarie Island declared a sanctuary since 1933, these penguins are now recovering some of their former numbers. The island is now a scientific station manned by Australian National Research Expeditions, and special permission must be obtained to go ashore there.

We mention these facts because it is important that human visitors to such sanctuaries during the breeding season should be controlled by appointed guides. The photographer or other curious well-meaning observer who walks through a crowded penguin rookery or ternery opens a passage for the swift attack of egg- and chick-stealing predators. After several such disturbances by jaywalking tourists there is likely to be a serious fall in breeding success which could end in the desertion of the site by its birds. Fortunately penguins have been given complete protection in Antarctica under an international agreement; observers are now required to do their observing from the perimeter of the rookery.

The Home Life of Penguins

Warmly clad in their wind- and water-proofed coats, penguins spend most of the year, and obtain all their food by, swimming and diving. They are essentially gregarious, and even at sea – on the principle, evidently, of the survival value of numbers – penguins crowd together to round up and feed on their plankton and squid food, more easily found with so many of them searching. As on land, predators have less chance of success in attacking the mob than the lone bird. If you see a solitary penguin, it is usually too weak to keep up with the flock, and will soon be mopped up by a scavenging predator. Their hesitant behaviour in approaching or leaving the land is an interesting mixture of instinctive fear and learning. Afraid of being attacked by lurking leopard seals and other aquatic enemies, they push and jostle closely together until one or two of the more courageous (desperate

Penguins

Left The smallest penguin – the Galapagos, *Spheniscus mendiculus*, survives on these equatorial islands in small numbers only – at the limit of heat tolerance for a penguin. Although the sea here is relatively cool where the Humboldt current washes the southern isles of this archipelago, the Galapagos Penguin avoids the noonday heat by being largely nocturnal and nesting in burrows in the lava rock. Note the marine iguana, a harmless seaweed-eating companion.

to feed in the sea or return to the nest) leap, whereupon the whole flotilla will rush to follow. Spectacular vertical jumps of up to two metres are made to gain a rock or ice ledge when leaving the water.

Healthy penguins exhibit great curiosity about each other's movements, even away from their nesting area. If one begins to stroll along a beach, the rest of an idle group will follow. The human observer who sits quietly by may soon be approached and investigated, even poked by a sharp enquiring bill. Follow-the-leader doggedly is an ingrained, partly learned habit of some importance in penguins, which often have to travel scores of kilometres over Antarctic snow and ice between sea and rookery. Orientation tests have shown that Adelie Penguins, *Pygoscelis adeliae*, experimentally released on the featureless ice plateau of Antarctica, far inland, were able to start homewards in a coastwise direction so long as the position of the sun was visible. If the sky was overcast the penguins wandered around or went to sleep and waited for the sky to clear. Two out of five Adelie Penguins taken by air and liberated 3,800km along the coast returned to the breeding grounds in ten months. Allowing half of each day for rest and feeding, this means an average of about 1km per hour, an astonishing record for a bird unable to fly!

There is a critical period of up to four weeks when penguins will not voluntarily enter the sea. Moulting at the end of the breeding season, they sit around silently on the land looking, and probably feeling, very miserable. Their feathers fall out rapidly, destroying their body insulation. However they usually lay up body fat for this long fast, and provided they do not move about much, and as long as strong winds do not blow away the old feathers, these remain clinging to the tips of the newly emerging downy feathers of the winter coat to keep the moulting bird reasonably warm. A moulting bird forced by accident to enter the water soon becomes sodden and will die of chill if it cannot quickly get back ashore. Hole-nesting penguins (Blue, *Eudyptula minor*, and Magellan, *Spheniscus magellanicus*) retire to their dens or other dry cover for the whole of this dangerous period.

Social and sexual behaviour in penguins follows the general pattern of seabirds described in the last chapter: mature males arrive first to claim a nesting territory and advertise, vocally and by display, for a mate. Pairs recognise each other by voice, and remain mated for life by their faithfulness to the same nesting site. Divorce is usually the result of an accident, such as the loss of an egg or chick early in the season. In his admirable studies of penguins, Bernard Stonehouse remarks that there is a bizarre, almost surrealist air of irrelevance and makeshift in their behaviour patterns, which are innate and evolved by the trial and error of natural selection to meet their average survival needs. But he admits they are difficult for man to study sensibly and objectively: 'They fight over territories, steal from the neighbours, beat their wives and bully their children. What further proof do we need that, deep down inside, they are just like you and me?'

Below The Peruvian Penguin, *S. humboldti*, is close cousin to two other *Spheniscus* penguins breeding in South America, and to the Jackass Penguin, *S. demersus*, of South Africa. All four wear the distinctive black horseshoe ring on the white breast and bray like a jackass. The Peruvian nests along the Humboldt current coast of western South America as far south as southern Chile, where it overlaps with the Magellan *S. magellanicus* of Tierra del Fuego and the Falklands. Clearly this *Spheniscus* genus originated in a common ancestor from the far south, swept north on the chill currents from the Antarctic Ocean which bring the plankton-rich water to the west coast of South America and South Africa.

Distribution

From their southern origin in Gondwanaland the penguins have diversified into about seventeen true species, to exploit fully the many ecological (food and geographical) niches of the lower levels of the seafood chain – the abundant plankton, squid and little fishes. How soon this speciation took place we do not know, but it is suggested that, in accordance with Bergmann's Rule (body-size of a related or sub-species increases with the decreasing mean temperature of its habitat), the larger and best adapted to cold during the late glacial epochs remained closest to the ice. Large bodies retain heat better than small ones because they have less surface area relative to bulk. Roughly this is so; the largest

penguin, the one-metre-plus tall Emperor, *Aptenodytes forsteri*, actually breeds on the ice in winter, while the two smallest, the Little, Blue or Fairy Penguin (only 40cm from bill to tail tip) and the Galapagos species, *Spheniscus mendiculus* (50cm), are resident today in temperate seas, far from any ice. The theory is that, having swum so far north at the height of the most severe glaciation, these two little species never returned south again, but found an agreeable vacant niche in the warmer climate, following the reduction of the polar ice-cap and the considerable rise in sea-level. They adapted to the heat by becoming smaller, and also nocturnal when on land.

It is easy for us to imagine how the gale-driven currents of chill water which circle west to east around the Antarctic

continent, and are deflected in a northerly direction by the obstructive western coasts of South America, South Africa and Australia, carried with them the components of the Antarctic food-chain, from photo- and zooplankton to penguins, whales and fishes. They still do. The cold Humboldt current touches the southernmost islands of the Galapagos group isolated at the equator, laden with sea-food for the resident seals, marine iguanas, the Galapagos Penguin, *Spheniscus mendiculus*, the Flightless Cormorant, *Nannopterum harrisi*, the Waved Albatross, *Diomedea albatrus*, and other seabirds which we describe in later chapters. Nevertheless the Galapagos Penguin seems to be at the limit of heat tolerance when, at erratic intervals, a warm south-flowing current known as El Niño pushes the cold Humboldt water

away from the islands. Its numbers are comparatively low; about 3,000 birds. It lays two eggs in a hole in the lava rock at any time of the year. Depending on how abundant its fish food is for rearing a brood, it may breed twice in the same year. It moults after each nesting period, and thus may also moult twice in a year!

In the same family are three other *Spheniscus* penguins, like the Galapagos species each with black legs, crown and back; white brows and front collar; and the white breast with a characteristic black horseshoe across the breast, extending down the flanks. Two live farther south in the Humboldt current; the Peruvian, *S. humboldti* (68cm), haunts the guano-covered Bird Rocks of the Peruvian and Chilean coasts, now so denuded by man of the ancient deposits of guano that the penguins can no longer dig their nesting burrows, but must find cover in rock holes and caves. Most abundant and widely dispersed around the South American coast, from Valparaiso on the west side to the large colonies near the Valdez Peninsula on the east side, including Tierra del Fuego and the Falkland Islands, is *S. magellanicus*. Their huge colonies were once exploited and much reduced by visiting sealing crews; and as far back as the days when the Spanish conquistadors (and Francis Drake's buccaneering ships) visited this coast there are records of thousands of these penguins being slaughtered to provision vessels on their long sailing voyages. Under protection in the present century their numbers have increased to several million. Two eggs are laid in a burrow dug in sand, shingle and grassland close to the sea. Under live vegetation a hollow suffices. After nesting the adults moult, at which time (autumn) they are joined by non-breeders one or more years old which come ashore for the same purpose – as in all penguin colonies. Slightly smaller, the Jackass or Blackfoot Penguin, *S. demersus*, is resident along the southern shores of South Africa, washed by the cold Benguela current. It normally lays twice a year, in February and September, potentially an increase of four young annually. Despite this, however, their numbers are not large; around 100,000. Of late many have been washed ashore dying from the effects of waste oil discharged by ships rounding the Cape of Good Hope.

The Fairy Penguin of southern Australia is the Little Blue of New Zealand coasts, smallest of the world's penguins and

A get-together club of idle Magellan Penguins, *S. magellanicus*. Some may be 'off-duty' adults, with mates at nests in ground burrows and holes. Some may be non-breeders, immatures in full adult plumage at the sweethearting stage of getting to know each other, the colony and a prospective mate – just as in human society. (Falkland Islands.)

Penguins

The Jackass, Blackfoot or Cape Penguin, *Spheniscus demersus*, breeding on islands around the Cape of Good Hope, South Africa, is a favourite penguin for exhibition and breeding in zoological collections. Due to much oil pollution from large tankers passing that way, it is slowly decreasing in numbers.

very distinctive in colour, a brilliant metallic blue above, and white below, including the near-white legs (but the soles of the feet are black). As it is shy at sea, and strictly nocturnal on land, it is rarely seen close to – except at one Australian site, which must be unique. During the breeding season, what is called the 'evening parade' of Fairy Penguins coming ashore after dark, and waddling in file and group to their nesting burrows on Phillip Island, 70km south of Melbourne, is a tourist attraction seen by hundreds of visitors and well organised to disturb the birds as little as possible. At this 'Summerland' colony the penguins burrow in dunes fenced off from human activity where they have been studied for several years. There is competition for desirable nesting tunnels with the Short-tailed Shearwater or Muttonbird, *Puffinus tenuirostris*, in which the more powerful penguin generally wins. In one recorded instance a hatching muttonbird egg was pirated by a female Fairy who guarded the newly-hatched chick for a week until it died of starvation. Feeding techniques of the two species differ too widely: the young penguin thrusts its head deep into the parental throat at meal-times, but all young shearwaters and petrels are fed by adult regurgitation of partly digested food direct into the chick's bill, which is held cross-wise within the gape of the parent's open mouth.

In New Zealand this penguin has a reputation for nesting under the floors of seaside homes, the human occupants of which are unable to sleep because of the nocturnal braying courtship conversation, and later the wheezing cries of the hungry chicks – two normally being raised in this secure den. It will also nest under a garden shed, or in an enlarged rabbit burrow, and a favourite site is deep under a large clump of New Zealand flax (*Phormium*). More than in other penguins the moult is sudden, almost violent, the old coat shed so rapidly that the Blue Penguin temporarily becomes a different blue – from the lead-blue sheaths of newly-emerging feathers. Wisely it lies up deep in a dry hole – not usually its nesting burrow which, by the end of the breeding season, is insanitary with guano splashings, fleas and ticks. Contrast this behaviour with that of the Yellow-eyed Penguin, *Megadyptes antipodes*, which Eric and I found sitting about upright on top of the cliffs of Enderby Island in the sub-Antarctic Auckland Isles. This stalwart creature (a good

Penguins

76cm tall) stood immovably in the sunshine, ringed about with its falling feathers. Its silent dignity was impressive, far from the hurly-burly of the crowded colonies we had left behind in Antarctica and Macquarie Island. This fine penguin is found only on southern New Zealand shores as far north as Dunedin, where you may meet it close to the famous Taiaroa Head Royal Albatross, *Diomedea epomophora*, sanctuary. It lays two eggs in the same situations as the Fairy, but is partly diurnal, strolling in daylight between the sea and the sandy bluffs it burrows in.

How curious that the Royal Penguin, in common with the other five crested (*Eudyptes*) penguins inhabiting the sub-Antarctic – Macaroni, *Eudyptes chrysolophus*, Erect-crested, *E. sclateri*, Rockhopper, Snares Island, *E. robustus*, and Fiordland, *E. pachyrhynchus* – lays two eggs which, like the ears of Edward Lear's Man of Devizes, are 'of different sizes: the one that was small was no good at all . . .' etc. It is the first-laid that is too small, and is no good; it is usually ejected from the nest a few days after the second and larger egg is laid. Should the second be lost by accident soon after it is laid, the first may be incubated, but produces a dwarf chick with small chance of survival. We see here, evidently, evolution towards a one-egg clutch?

More truly adapted to Antarctica, the three *Pygoscelis* penguins have lately been much studied in the large colonies we visited, from the Antarctic Peninsula south to the Ross Sea. The species are the same size, but very different in appearance. Of these the most cold-resistant is the Adelie Penguin, which we found nesting around Shackleton's historic hut under Mt Erebus on Ross Island. This is as far south as any flightless bird can breed in summer. But this hardy penguin returns from wintering in the pack-ice long before there is open water close to home. Thoroughly insulated against the bitter frost in its thick plumage (even the short beak is well-feathered), and plump with good feeding, it marches many kilometres over the ice and through snow blizzards to reach by October its well-remembered rookeries, which are usually in fairly windswept, open sites. Here on fine days it begins to rebuild a nest of small stones which will serve to keep the two eggs (they are chalky-white, sometimes with a greenish cast) above meltwater levels later in the summer. The mature pair spend up to a month at this, courting, stealing stones from neighbours, and making a great din in defending their territory. As soon as the female has laid the eggs, the male takes them over and incubates for about a fortnight, while she toddles off to sea to recuperate: she has lost a lot of weight fasting and producing the eggs. She returns to relieve him for a short spell half-way through the five week incubation period, and after recuperating at sea he returns to complete the job. Mother Adelie now reappears with a stomach full of krill, and the nestlings are fed once daily at first. At three weeks old they are strong enough to join a nursery or crèche with other chicks. This enables both parents to go fishing and

Right The large handsome Yellow-eyed Penguin, *Megadyptes antipodes*, 76 cm tall, breeds only in the South Island of New Zealand and as far south as Campbell Island. On our visit to Enderby Island in the Aucklands group in March it was standing around in the open, deep in moult and almost comatose. A dignified-looking species, it is more solitary than other penguins, rearing one or two chicks in a burrow under sub-Antarctic scrub.

Far left On Macquarie Island we found the Royal Penguin, *Eudyptes schlegeli*, well recovered from the serious persecution by sealing gangs in the last century and early in the present, when it was boiled down in iron vats for the sake of its fat which was rendered into oil. Unique to Macquarie, the Royals are now estimated to be two million birds strong.

Left This Macaroni Penguin, *E. chrysolophus*, recognisable by its stouter bill and golden eyebrow plumes, has somehow become attached to a breeding group of Rockhopper Penguins, *E. chrysocome*, in the Falkland Islands, where both species commonly nest. Compare eyebrow style with the Rockhopper Penguin.

Penguins

so bring back larger croploads to satisfy the chick's increased appetite. The ice is now leaving the shore, and the sea swarms with zooplankton. Generally there are a few adults (some are non-breeders which have come in late) forming a guard, ready to attack a marauding skua, gull or sheathbill. A healthy chick quickly learns how to lunge at such an enemy.

The Chinstrap Penguin, *Pygoscelis antarctica*, comically resembles a London policeman in its black 'helmet' with a thin black chinstrap below the white face. If you approach too near its stone-platform nest it will charge you at the run, pecking and beating your legs with its flailing flippers. Possibly 14 million inhabit remote Zavodovski Island in the South Sandwich group. We encountered smaller colonies, some mixed with Adelies and Gentoos, farther south on islands of the Antarctic Peninsula, but not on the mainland of the frozen continent. The Gentoo by contrast is comparatively timid. Although it will nest in the open it also likes to lay its two eggs near some object such as a rock, a whale bone or a clump of tussock, sometimes on the crown of the latter – as at Macquarie, South Georgia and the Falkland Islands. Where all three *Pygoscelis* penguins co-exist, they do so because they seem to exploit different levels and sizes of their common, abundant plankton food. Judging by the colours of the guano you will see splashed around the nest and upon the throat of an adult feeding a chick, the Gentoo brings home more squid than the Chinstrap or Adelie, which both produce a rich red waste from crustacean krill.

Finally the two largest: the stately handsome (*Aptenodytes*) Emperor and King Penguins, with even more remarkable life histories; linked as squid-fishers, but well apart in habitat. Both incubate the single egg *on top of the feet*, where it is held in place and kept at blood heat against the naked skin, hidden beneath a kind of sporran or pouch of feathered belly skin. The incubating adult is able to shuffle around holding the egg securely in this fashion, which it does as necessary to avoid bad weather and wet places. There is no nest and no territory within the colony, for which reason these penguins are more peaceful and have gentler voices. They are very sociable, and will huddle together to conserve heat in blizzard and frost.

The King prefers to breed on sub-Antarctic islands, selecting roomy raised beaches, tussock plateaux, and sometimes muddy deltas where meltwater flows in summer. In this comparatively mild climate (Macquarie, South Georgia,

Falklands) it has easy access to the sea even in winter – and needs it, owing to its protracted rearing season which results in both chicks and adults being present at colonies throughout the year. By laying alternately, early and late, the King Penguin has achieved a unique breeding rota, fitting two breeding cycles into three calendar years. Although it comes ashore in the (October) spring it is so long over courtship (a month or more), incubation (54 days), and rearing that the bleak sub-Antarctic winter overtakes the young bird at the crèche stage. It is by then well covered with down, almost as large as its parents, and very fat. It is now obliged to spend the five months of winter living on this stored fat; the parents return to feed it only at rare intervals of nearly a month. Not until spring returns will they freely bring in the now more plentiful squid, enabling the chick to make up its lost weight.

It completes feathering, and finally takes to the sea when about eleven months old. The adults must now moult; after which they will court and mate again too late in the summer to rear more than two chicks in three seasons. Late-born chicks often die of cold and starvation.

At four feet (122cm) the majestic Emperor is one-quarter taller than the King Penguin, and weighs up to 45kg on coming ashore to breed. Where this might be was not discovered until, in 1902, Edward Wilson, artist-doctor on Scott's Antarctic wintering parties, was first to find its eggs as told in Cherry-Garrard's dramatic story *The Worst Journey in the World* (1922). It is now known that there are about a quarter of a million adult birds scattered around the Antarctic continent between 66°S and 78°S, in some two dozen colonies ranging in size from 300 birds to 100,000 strong.

Less than 300 may not be successful for huddling together in temperatures often below −40°C, and winds reaching speeds of up to 180kph. For this amazing creature comes from a summer of wandering in the pack-ice – no-one quite knows where – to seek a partner just as the Antarctic sea-ice is beginning to freeze again in March. With an unerring sense of direction they march in single file to the familiar nursery site, usually on new sea-ice, attached to the land, fairly level, and perhaps protected by ice-covered rocks or pressure ridges which may break the full force of a winter blizzard.

Marking has proved that partners remain faithful, by voice recognition, although there is occasional bigamy due to there being about 10 per cent more females than males. There is of course no food available: the sea is covered by the rapidly extending winter ice for many kilometres north-

wards; but the adults are too excited with courtship activities, which last well over a month. They freely eat snow. When at last the female lays the large egg (0.5kg) in May, the male eagerly beaks it into his belly pouch. Exhausted and starving, having lost perhaps half her weight during the long love-making and egg-building period, she trundles off, now and then tobogganing down slopes, with the other females (egg-laying is closely synchronous as a result of the mass stimulation of display in a large colony). The sea-ice is now solid for perhaps more than 100km from the breeding site, though there are usually tide-cracks and some breathing holes kept open by the overwintering Antarctic seals. Like these, Emperor Penguins will dive to feed at considerable depths. Harrison and Kooyman (1971), attaching depth-recorders to Emperor Penguins at their Ross Island colony, were able to register 'vertical plunges, usually of a group of up to 50 birds, and they ranged in depth from 45 to 265m'.

The females are in no hurry to return, in fact they rarely do so before the egg hatches. Meanwhile, over this period of courtship, followed by incubation, the males endure a fast of about four months through the long midwinter polar night. During the frequent blizzards they form dense huddles, each bird facing inwards with its body tight against that of its neighbours, a solid testudo resisting weather and conserving heat. On calm days they resume individual safety distance and air and preen themselves. If his partner has not returned before the egg hatches, the male, although almost emaciated (he loses about half his body weight), is still able to give his child some fluid nourishment from the mucus secretions of his stomach – if it demands food by whining a few days after it has absorbed the egg-yolk it is born with. When mother arrives she is fat, and her stomach laden with enough food to last the chick several weeks while father goes off on a long march to the sea.

We now see the advantage of winter breeding. By the time (about September) the Emperor chick is old enough to leave the pouch and form its own huddles in 'kindergarten crèches', the winter sea-ice is beginning to break out and both parents are now free to go fishing, making shorter marches to obtain larger, more frequent meals for their child. They call it out from the crèche by voice recognition. At six months the youngster, an engaging creature with black eyes in a white facial rosette, is almost ready to accompany its parents to sea. Sometimes the ice-nursery itself breaks away

The breast of one King Penguin, *Aptenodytes patagonicus*, in this idle group carries a recent wound, probably the result of an attack by a leopard seal, or by an orca (killer whale), two principal predators of Antarctic and sub-Antarctic penguins feeding at sea.

Penguins

An elegant party of off-duty King Penguins, *Aptenodytes patagonicus*, parade at Macquarie Island beach, looking svelte and handsome in freshly moulted plumage after the rigours of the long breeding season, of perhaps more than a year, are over.

and drifts out to sea. The January summer holidays have arrived; there is nothing to do but moult and feed, and play for the youngsters who learn to perfect their swimming and diving. They have hitherto had few enemies except winter cold and rough weather, which has nevertheless saved them from the several predators which trouble the summer-breeding penguins. Thus, despite being the largest penguin, the Emperor, by breeding over the winter, completes the reproductive cycle within ten months. Theoretically there is time for it to lay on enough fat to be in prime condition to mate and rear progeny annually, once the bird has reached sexual maturity. First breeding in this large penguin takes place at about six years of age.

Longevity

How long may penguins live, if they survive the hazards of their natural predators – leopard seals and other enemies at sea, and on land, as described later, skua, gull and sheathbill? In captivity they have lived more than 30 years. Occasionally a live or dead penguin (and also a lone seal) has been found far inland in Antarctica, as if each creature had wandered there deliberately, to die of old age, no longer interested in food or companionship. It is true of many seabirds that, if they are ill, some will seek to isolate themselves, to await death which comes to all living things. A late scientist friend of ours, Robert Cushman Murphy, in his charming book *Logbook for Grace*, dedicated to his wife, relates how, at South Georgia in January 1913:

> 'Near the summit of a coastal hill I came across a lonely pond in a hollow of ice-cracked stones. Several sick and drooping penguins were standing at the edge of this pool of snow water, which was ten or twelve feet deep. Then, with a tingling of my spine, I perceived that the bottom was strewn, layer upon layer, with the bodies of Gentoo penguins that had outlived the perils of the sea to accomplish the rare feat among wild animals of dying a natural death. By hundreds, possibly by thousands, they lay all over the bed of the cold tarn, flippers outstretched and breasts reflecting blurred gleams of white. Safe at last from sea leopards in the ocean and from skuas ashore, they took their endless rest; for decades, perhaps for centuries, the slumberers would undergo no change in their frigid tomb.'

CHAPTER 3
The Petrels

Albatrosses

Like the penguins, the large family of petrels (Procellariidae – tube-nosed) probably originated in the southern hemisphere in ancient Gondwanaland. During the late glacial epochs, some evidently moved north to warmer latitudes. Of these, three species of albatross, those most aerial and graceful gliders, crossed the equator to colonise the North Pacific. Two species, the Laysan, *Diomedea immutabilis*, and the Black-footed, *Diomedea nigripes*, are still relatively plentiful in the windy plankton-and-squid-rich Hawaiian seas. Fate has been less kind to the third North Pacific species, the Short-tailed Albatross, *Diomedea albatrus*. Only about 250 individuals now remain, with breeding confined to the Ja-

panese volcanic islet of Toroshima where about 60 pairs attempt to breed annually. One species of albatross settled in the Galapagos, on Hood Island, where about 12,000 pairs now breed annually and which Eric had the pleasure of visiting. This is the Waved Albatross, *Diomedea irrorata*, which feeds principally in the cool waters of the Humboldt current to the south. A few pairs now breed on Las Platas Island, off Ecuador.

The long narrow wings of albatrosses are adapted to gliding at high speeds (up to 100kph) but almost effortlessly, on strong winds above the turbulent seas of their wide ocean range. They have a greater capacity for dynamic soaring at speed than any other bird, which can be seen when one flies close to a ship with never a flap of the wings. It takes advantage of the wind deflected from waves or the side of the ship, gathering speed as it glides downwards to within a metre of the water, then swings up to about 20m, losing speed as it rises, before the diving glide which renews full speed. Thus it progresses faster than any steaming ship, and in order to remain with the ship it glides in wide ellipses around the vessel. It flies much too fast to take food on the wing. It must alight on the water, normally taking squid at or near the surface, making short dives as necessary to hook food with the forceps of its long bill. As squid rise to the surface at night, this explains why one seldom sees an albatross feeding – but it will alight to grab any meat or fish garbage thrown overboard from the ship's galley.

In dead calms the larger albatrosses have difficulty in

Left Virtually the same size as the Wanderer, the Royal Albatross, *Diomedea epomophora*, is confined as a breeder to sub-Antarctic islands off New Zealand, and one headland near Dunedin – at the latter it has been intensively studied for half a century. Both Royal and Wanderer take so long to complete courtship, incubation and successful rearing of their single replacement that breeding takes place only once every two years.

Above This Wandering Albatross, *D. exulans*, greeted us as soon as our ship left Tierra del Fuego for the Drake Passage. The largest albatross, with wingspan of up to 324cm (nearly 11ft), it breeds on many sub-Antarctic islands around the world, gliding with scarcely a beat of the long narrow wings, uplifted by the incessant westerly winds.

rising in flight on such long narrow wings, and after a period of night feeding, when they are glutted with food, and perhaps also moulting, they can be taken in handnets from a fast motorboat. Off the Australian coasts, banding of albatrosses has been carried out at sea with interesting results; recovery of Wandering Albatrosses, *Diomedea exulans*, and giant petrels marked on sub-Antarctic breeding grounds proves that there is a circumpolar, west-wind-assisted migration of these species when they are not nesting.

Seven species of albatross breed on the southern shores and sub-Antarctic islands of New Zealand, of which the Royal, equal in size to the Wanderer, is unique in nesting on the mainland at Taiaroa Head near the port of Dunedin. Both breed on the Campbell and Auckland Islands. It is an agreeable experience to walk slowly, or preferably creep on hands and knees, up to a nesting Wandering or Royal Albatross, and sit within touching distance, so tame are these great birds when incubating, or brooding a downy young chick. The adult may clapper its bill at you, but no more vigorously than it does in greeting its mate. You feel that aggression would be quite out of place in such a handsome and dignified-looking bird.

The male arrives first to prepare the home in both species. Bill-clappering and wing-waving ceremonies may last for a month before the single egg is laid. Incubation in long shifts by each partner occupies around 78 days. The downy chick is brooded until it acquires a second growth of down, enabling it to keep warm at four to five weeks old, when both parents

are away at sea collecting food. It is now less often visited and fed, remaining in the nest for eight months (Royal) or nine months (Wanderer); thus it is overtaken by the bitter sub-Antarctic winter and may be temporarily snowed under during this longest fledging period of any young bird.

A whole year has passed in the reproductive cycle, and the adults are in no condition to attempt breeding again until they have moulted and had a restful sabbatical year at sea. Meanwhile those that have just completed such a holiday will be returning to refurbish old nests, while there may still be fledglings on other nests just preparing to leave the nest site in the same October-November spring. Since these large albatrosses (and perhaps also some of the larger mollymawks) only breed once in two years, and so do not start to maintain their numbers until sexually mature at six to ten years old, they must be quite long-lived. Estimates range up to 50 years.

The two great albatrosses, as the Wanderer and Royal are sometimes called, select an open space for nesting – with a slope downhill, clear of other nests, for taxiing into the wind for take-off. Because of their long wings and poor powers of walking, all albatrosses prefer to site their nests in windy places. Building on steep slopes and cliffs, the two handsome sooty albatrosses and the five southern mollymawks – Black-browed, *Diomedea melanophris*, Buller's, *D. bulleri*, White-capped or Shy, *D. cauta*, Yellow-nosed, *D. chlororhynchos*, and Grey-headed, *D. chrysostoma* – select windswept places where they can hover in the breeze and drop accurately on,

Left Only one colony of some 12,000 pairs of the Waved Albatross, *Diomedea irrorata*, survives in the Galapagos Islands, the bulk nesting on Hood Island, where Eric took these photographs.

Below Courtship of the Wandering Albatross, *Diomedea exulans*. The pair advance with raised wings and rattle their wings together, St Georgia.

Overleaf Albatrosses do not seem at home at the Equator, but this species (*D. irrorata*) finds its food southward, soaring in the windy zone above the upwelling waters of the cool Humboldt current.

Phoebetria palpebrata, the Light-mantled Sooty Albatross, is perfectly at home in a rough breeze in the Ross Sea. With its narrow wings and long pointed tail it is one of the most graceful and aerial of seabirds. It prefers to nest rather solitarily on steep cliffs from which it can launch easily into the wind, as at Macquarie and other sub-Antarctic islands.

or near, the nest.

The mollymawks build a substantial nest of mud and tussock, adding to it during the shared incubation – a displacement activity which does help to maintain the structure above ground-level dangers, rain from sudden cloudbursts, and squirts of guano from neighbours (Black-browed Mollymawks usually nest very close together). On average incubation takes 70 days, and the chick spends about 120 days in the nest; total reproductive period, adding a month for courtship ceremonies, occupies about two-thirds of the year so there is time to moult and fatten before the following spring. Probably some pairs breed annually and some, the less experienced younger adults, miss out a year, enjoying a holiday wandering – as mollymawks do – many hundreds of miles northward in winter. Occasionally a Black-

browed has crossed the equator and lived for several years consorting with North Atlantic Gannets (13 all told between 1963 and 1968 at British and Icelandic (Westmann) sites). One such visitor lived in the northern hemisphere for 34 summers, up to 1894. Recently (1982) one has built a nest at a gannetry in the Shetland Islands.

At Macquarie we met the beautiful Light-mantled Sooty Albatross, *Phoebetria palpebrata*, at the nest, having studied its graceful flight swooping around our ship farther south. With its dark eye circled with a white ring, chocolate plumage and long tail it is most attractive. But at the nest its downy white-cheeked half-grown chick firmly drove us away with a well-aimed jet of smelly oil from the opened mouth. This albatross prefers to site its nest well apart from the next, and often solitarily on an inaccessible cliff.

Fulmars

The so-called giant petrels are the largest of the fulmar petrels, and notable for their huge and formidable bill with its elongated nasal tube. The birds' ugly faces, and their ravenous habit of gorging on dead animals at sea, and scavenging behind whaleships and at meatwork outfalls, have earned them the names stinker, black molly, glutton, etc. The giant petrel has the same defensive habit of squirting stinking stomach oil at the intruder as the other, smaller fulmars. In the air it is a graceful glider, following ships for hours in every part of the Roaring Forties latitude south to the Antarctic continent. We have seen both species of giant petrel. The Southern Giant Petrel, *Macronectes giganteus*, is a semi-resident on the Antarctic coast. It is slightly larger than

The Petrels

the Northern Giant Petrel, *Macronectes halli*, which is confined mostly to sub-Antarctic islands and differs mainly in its polymorphic plumages; the pale form is mostly white. There are ecological differences in nesting and egg-laying dates. The Southern Giant Petrel prefers open headlands where it nests in closer groups on more exposed ground; the Northern Giant Petrel is more solitary, building its untidy nest of any handy debris close to cover of vegetation or rock. Both species attend the seasonal whelping of seals in order to devour the placenta, and even attack unguarded new-born pups.

Blundering when it walks on land, the giant petrel nevertheless is able to attack and kill with one blow of its powerful bill any lone, sick or unguarded penguin chicks, even those of the Emperor making their way to the sea for the first time in the summer. It quickly disembowels its victim, tearing at the viscera in competition with other giant petrels, and perhaps skuas. Like vultures these scavengers will thrust their head and neck into the carcase of a seal until they are dyed red with blood. Yet at the nest the giant petrel is as faithful and home-caring as all the petrels, penguins and gulls are. The male has a rather peacock-like display, fanning his tail in the air to advertise his desire to mate. After agreeing on a nest site and mating, the pair go away to sea to feed for about two weeks. They return for the egg-laying, the male taking the first incubation shift of several days, then the female takes hers; and the usual pattern of petrel nidification is followed – sharing, with shifts of fasting at the nest

alternating with feasting at sea. Incubation lasts about 60 days. The down-covered nestling is jealously guarded for up to a month by one or other parent; the off-duty partner meanwhile collects food to bring home to the chick – never to the adult. The adolescent, finally deserted, takes off after a brief fast when it is about 100 days old. For the next three to five years it will roam the southern latitudes widely, perhaps circumnavigating the world several times within the 30°–60°S parallels. On its first return to land, invariably close to where it was hatched, the male will spend another year or two finding a mate and a place in the community before a permanent summer home is established, shared with the female giant petrel who has responded to his courtship antics in a suitably submissive manner.

This partnership pattern is followed by the two much smaller fulmar petrels, but over a much shorter period. They are extremely elegant and tireless gliders in flight; white-breasted with pearl-grey wings which use the air currents of cliff, wave or ship with hardly a flicker of the planing, stiffly-held quills. Both species are wanderers of polar and sub-polar seas, nesting on bare ledges and open places on preferably steep cliffs. The Southern Fulmar, *Fulmarus glacialoides*, also known as the Silver-grey Petrel, breeds around the whole Antarctic continent and its islands within range of the pack-ice. The Northern Fulmar, *F. glacialis*, is even more numerous along all Arctic coasts in summer. We found it the most abundant bird at sea around Spitsbergen (Svalbard), Jan Mayen, Iceland, and on the Pacific side in the Aleutian and

Left The Shy or White-headed Albatross, *Diomedea cauta*, which appeared at the same time, competing for our fish bait, and giving us a nice contrast in the bill colour – obvious in these pictures. The Shy Albatross, when not breeding on the Auckland Islands, and islets around Tasmania, wanders over the whole of the sub-Antarctic Ocean, including the Indian sector.

Above Well-named from its dark eyebrows, the Black-browed Albatross, *D. melanophris* – a graceful glider, but a poor walker.

Bering Seas. There is a darker or bluer phase in the highest latitudes of the Atlantic; but it was replaced by the pale form as the *Lindblad Explorer* moved south across the Arctic Circle.

Studying the Northern Fulmar at sea from a trawler at the Rockall Bank, far west of the Outer Hebrides, it seemed clear to us why, during the present century, the bird has spread rapidly south to breed on cliffs along European Atlantic coasts as far south as France. At each first loud clank of the winch used to haul in the trawl at four-hour intervals throughout the day and night, about 2,000 fulmars would congregate at our ship's side, to glut themselves on the steady flow of fish offal and unsaleable small fish trickling from the scuppers as the crew rapidly gutted the catch. This took about half an hour to complete, by which time the first-comers were too gorged to fly easily, while those arriving late and not satisfied would fly off to another trawler fishing these fertile banks. As there were at that time (1947–50) many hundreds of trawlers fishing within the 100-fathom line along all ice-free North Atlantic coasts, these ocean-going wandering birds enjoyed almost unlimited access to an abundant food supply, for the trouble of a brief gliding search for the next fishing trawler hauling its nets. We should perhaps note that in the present decade, with overfishing by modern methods including large trawling and ringnetting gear, almost no waste is today thrown overboard: it is processed aboard, or put under hatches for processing ashore, to be sold as fish meal or fertiliser. Even plankton and shrimp krill is now being swept from the sea, creating food shortage problems for some seabirds (page 154). There may soon be a decline in the Northern Fulmar population.

Right Buller's Mollymawk, *D. bulleri*. The angle of light in this flight picture over-emphasises the dark hood, the crown being almost white – but not as pure white as the crown of the Shy or White-headed Albatross.

Below The Black-browed Albatross breeds in gregarious groups on many sub-Antarctic islands as far north as the Falklands, where this picture was taken. It selects a windswept position, such as a headland, to build a solid raised cup-nest, from which it can lift in flight, or alight on by hovering in the wind.

Cape Petrel or Pintado

One of the most numerous southern cold-water petrels of medium size (rather smaller than the Southern Fulmar with which it associates at sea), the Pintado, *Daption capensis*, has a similar breeding habitat, selecting niches in high cliffs to rear its single chick, which has a sooty-coloured down (the fulmar chick has white down). Normally the Pintado feeds by swimming at the surface, paddling with its webbed feet far apart to draw zooplankton towards its dabbling bill. This is broad, with a ridge of horny lamellae which retains the food while straining the water, as in the six species of the related prion petrels or whalebirds (*Pachyptila*).

Because so many medium to small species of ocean-going petrels are confusing to the human observer at first, the sealers and whalers of the last century gave them distinguishing names. We have already referred to stinker and black molly for the giant petrel. The smaller albatrosses were dubbed 'mollies' or mollymawks. Other names include Cape Pigeon for Pintado because this bird was first encountered in numbers when the sailing ships were rounding the Cape of Good Hope – where it is still abundant; and whalebirds for prions, also known as icebirds and firebirds because in the ice-troubled seas where men hunted whales and seals these little petrels were attracted by lights and fires as they returned home to their burrows on sub-Antarctic islands at

night. Fulmars and Pintado, breeding in the open on cliff ledges, can defend their egg or young chick by aggressively lunging, and spitting the evil-smelling stomach-oil at an unwelcome visitor. The small prions must come ashore, and swiftly enter their burrows in the sloping screes at night, to avoid marauding gulls, skuas and sheathbills. Even so, where they nest in huge colonies, as at South Georgia, the Falklands, and several New Zealand islands where the midsummer night is not dark enough, the prions suffer heavy casualties entering or leaving their nesting holes. At sea, prions fly with great speed, easily avoiding predators. They feed on krill, diving briefly, skimming the surface with the specialised bill, squirting out water and retaining food.

Left A small albatross, Buller's Mollymawk, *D. bulleri*, nests only on the Snares and Chatham Islands southward of New Zealand in cool sub-Antarctic water of the 'Roaring Forties' latitude. It eagerly attended our small boat off Stewart Island, coming close to the bait of fishguts which we threw to it.

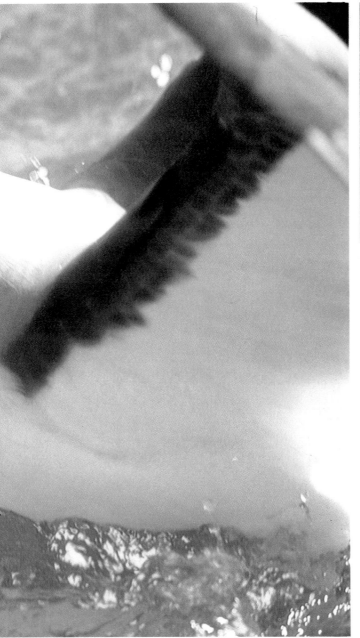

Above Giant petrels compete for fish offal thrown overboard near the Snares, isolated islets south of New Zealand. They are ruthless scavengers of flesh from any source, including meatworks and sewer outfalls, the carcasses and afterbirth of seals and any small seabird they can surprise on sea or land. Yet at home they are model parents, sharing incubation and tenderly caring for their single chicks. The northern species, *Macronectes halli*, breeds on the Snares and other islands north of 55°S – the Antarctic Convergence; the southern *M. giganteus* (which has a white phase) breeds in groups on exposed headlands southwards, including the Antarctic mainland. This huge petrel walks awkwardly on land, preferring to nest where a strong wind assists take-off.

Prions are pretty to watch in their soft blue upper plumage as they circle the ship, feeding on plankton disturbed and brought to the surface by bows and propellor in the cold southern ocean. Here we frequently met the Blue Petrel, *Halobaena caerulea*, so alike in colour and size to the prions. But for the fact that the Blue has a white tip, and the prion a black tip, to the tail, you could hardly distinguish them at sea. The Blue is really a small gadfly petrel which, like the prions, visits its burrow by night for the same reason, and sometimes on the same sub-Antarctic island.

Loveliest and most remarkable of the Antarctic petrels is the Snow Petrel, *Pagodroma nivea*, pure white save for a dark bill, eyes and feet. We found it frequently resting on icebergs, where it blended with this white background so well. It

Top Defensive behaviour of Northern Fulmars, *Fulmarus glacialis*, spitting oil at intruder. Orkneys, where some nest in derelict buildings.

Above St Kildan with his catch of Fulmars taken early 1920s.

Right A pair of Northern (Atlantic) Fulmars, *Fulmarus glacialis*, at the nest in the Shetlands. In 100 years it has spread from the Arctic and St Kilda, to cover most cliffs and islands around the British Isles and the north coast of France, a spectacular increase (see page 76).

breeds in small colonies in niches in steep cliffs and screes, often far inland in Antarctica. So too does the quite distinctive Antarctic Petrel, *Thalassoica antarctica*, brown with white rump and wing-edges, a larger bird which has few, but massive, colonies on certain Antarctic cliffs, some as much as 300km from the sea.

All these petrels have the same general breeding pattern, already outlined several times: but because of the short summer in Antarctica, egg-laying and hatching times are synchronous to within a few days. There is abundant food for these krill-eating birds as soon as the young appear; and before summer ends with February they are fledged and away to sea, for the usual few years of adolescent wandering.

Shearwaters

Some 54 species of these medium-large to medium-small tube-nosed birds have been rather loosely divided into shearwater (*Puffinus*) and gadfly (*Pterodroma*) groups by taxonomists who still occasionally revise their scientific names. Most of the smaller species are not easy to study as they are nocturnal in visiting their remote nesting islands and cliffs. Typically they mate for life once a burrow has been established, and here the males generally arrive first. After mating, the female feeds at sea for several days before returning to lay the one white egg, which the male incubates for the first shift. The shared work of raising a replacement is accomplished in alternating shifts of several days during the

The Petrels

rather long incubation period, up to 60 days, and the still longer period of dependence of the chick (100 days or more in the nest).

At chill sub-Arctic and sub-Antarctic breeding sites this period is strictly over the warmer months, and annual. But in temperate and tropical latitudes certain petrels may breed at any time, evidently because there is competition for the most desirable sites. In the tropics this may be so intense on certain favoured islands free of introduced predators (cats, rats, mongooses) that the more dominant of two petrel species will breed at the optimum period for food-gathering to promote successful egg-production and feeding of young. The other petrel adapts to breeding in the rest of the year.

During our visit to camp on the remote Selvagen Islands, north of the Canaries, we found an even more complicated

competition for undercover nesting sites. The large and powerful Mediterranean (or Cory's) Shearwater, *Calonectris diomedea*, occupied all the larger holes, and could be seen in the more exposed ones incubating in a good light; it has no enemies capable of tackling it save man. (The fledglings are collected for food by visiting Portuguese, who protect the adults on this island which they regard as their 'Cagarra farm' – so-named because of this shearwater's harsh call.) In smaller crevices, some at the rear of the Cagarra dens, the dainty Frigate or White-faced Petrel, *Pelagodroma marina*, might be nesting, as it was everywhere in the small burrows in the soil of the plateau of the island at the time of our visit in mid-July. In some of these burrows we found the charming Little Shearwater, *Puffinus assimilis*, indulging in courtship – no eggs or young as yet; while in others the Madeiran Petrel,

84

Oceanodroma castro, had just started to lay its egg. Discounting the Cory's Shearwater as overlord of all large holes, the numerous small tunnels and burrows in the soil and the smaller rock crevices of Grande Selvagen were successively occupied throughout the year by a fairly neat division into three periods of four-months: the White-faced Petrels occupy the honeycomb from April to July, the Madeiran Petrels from August to November, and the Little Shearwaters from December to March – the northern winter. We may note that the Little Shearwater elsewhere (for example in Australasia) is a winter breeder, often on islands where the White-faced Petrel is a summer nester.

Related species may apportion the year equally between them on the same island, each taking six months approximately to complete reproduction. At the Tristan da Cunha group in the South Atlantic, *Puffinus gravis*, the Great Shearwater, breeds in the summer from October to March, migrating north in the northern summer to feed off the Newfoundland fishing banks and across towards Rockall where we have watched it competing for trawler offal with other seabirds (page 76). The same burrows on Tristan may then be used by the winter-nesting Great-winged Petrel, *Pterodroma macroptera*, a slightly smaller bird.

Generally the numerous species of tube-nosed birds, from albatrosses and shearwaters to the tiny storm petrels, seem to be highly successful at present; which argues that their food must be abundant and efficiently collected. Also, from the competition for territory we have mentioned, there does not today seem to be an adequate number of suitable islands to nest upon that are free of lethal predators. Before man arrived

Preceding page The Cape Pigeon or Pintado, *Daption capense*, a more sub-Antarctic species, with a whitely mottled back and broader black tail band. This flock was feeding on krill in the Neumeyer Channel off the Antarctic Peninsula. Method of gathering food is to draw plankton towards its dipping bill, by 'marking time' with its paddling feet as it swims slowly forward.

Left We found this dainty, newly-fledged Fairy Prion, *Pachyptila turtur*, blown ashore on Stewart Island, evidently lately emerged from the burrow in which it was feeding on one of the nearby islets. Only 23cm (9 in) long, it is the smallest of eight prion species, sometimes called whalebirds because they feed on the planktonic krill in company with the whales who do the same. And, like the baleen whales, they scoop this food into a throat pouch, then expel the surplus water through sieve-like horny ridges (lamellae) along the edge of the bill, by pressure of the large fleshy tongue. On the wing they fly gracefully, easily eluding enemies, such as skuas and gulls, which attack prions when they come to land, entering or leaving their burrows on remote sub-Antarctic and southern ocean islands.

The Petrels

Left The beautiful pure white Snow Petrel, *Pagodroma nivea*, has dark eyes, bill and feet, mysterious birds to us as rare visitors to their chill habitat, gliding around like huge snowflakes, or perched upon icebergs. It is here seen in the Ross Sea. It nests on snow-bound cliffs, often far inland in Antarctica – as at King Edward VII Land, over 80km from the sea.

Above The Antarctic Petrel, *Thalassoica antarctica*, was our frequent companion at sea as the *Lindblad Explorer* ranged along the Antarctic coast. Well named, this hardy petrel haunts the limits of the floating pack-ice south of latitude 60° S. It feeds largely on the krill shrimp, *Euphausia superba*, and breeds on cliffs, often far inland. In size and general plumage pattern and colour it resembles the Cape Pigeon or Pintado.

to colonise so many, they were often crammed with seabirds, including many burrowing petrels. In those early centuries before man learned to sail the oceans, the petrel family must have been even more successful and numerous if we are to judge by the fact that a number were obliged (as we may speculate) to nest not only on mainland cliffs but also on the tops of high mountains because of the fierce competition for the more accessible small islands of the ocean. For instance in New Zealand, relatively lately colonised by man when the first Polynesians arrived about a thousand years ago, some of the large shearwaters were freely breeding inland on crags and mountain tops. One was the winter-breeding Great-winged Petrel (known in New Zealand as the Grey-faced), still nesting on steep seaward-facing crags, but now reduced largely to offshore islands. It is the 'titi' or 'muttonbird' eaten by the North Island Maori. On those same mountain tops and on one or two islands only a remnant is left of the summer-breeding Black Petrel, *Procellaria parkinsoni*, also a titi formerly collected by the Maori for food (when the fledglings were fat and deserted by their parents in the autumn). Even rarer today is the Westland Black Petrel, *Procellaria westlandica*, a fairly recent offshoot of the Black, but larger and breeding exclusively deep in the rainforest of the west coast of the South Island, in winter. Yet it was safe enough here until rats, ferrets, stoats and weasels were introduced into New Zealand about a century ago: they were brought in to control rabbits, but they preferred the more easily caught native birds! A sad tale, so often repeated as man and his predatory camp followers invaded the world's pristine shores and islands; we need not labour the point here, except as a lesson to emphasise the great need to preserve the few islands at present still free of such introductions – of which the worst are pigs, rats and mustelids, including mongoose. The Spanish galleons of the seventeenth century, discovering uninhabited Bermuda, subsequently provisioned their conquistadorial voyages with thousands of the shearwaters (especially Audubon's Shearwater, *Puffinus lherminieri*, and the Cahow) which yelled and flew over the anchorage each night, returning to their burrows. The Cahow, peculiar to Bermuda, was believed to have become extinct as early as

Right In the Ross Sea the Blue Petrel, *Halobaena caerulea*, looks small and very like one of the prions, in the evening glow of a sun which does not set at midsummer here. The black *v* of the blue wings of these fast-flying petrels is almost identical, but the tail of the Blue Petrel is distinctively white-tipped. It breeds on remote Antarctic cliffs and also on the Falklands.

The Petrels

Overleaf The large dark brown Wedge-tailed Shearwater, *P. pacificus*, roams the whole of the tropical Pacific and Indian Oceans. This one was surprised by flashlight outside its burrow on the Seychelles. All shearwaters recognise their partners by voice in the darkness of night and burrow, and have similar breeding habits: shared incubation lasting about 50 days, the young bird remaining in the burrow for about 100 days.

Below Leach's Petrel, *Oceanodroma leucorhoa* – adult and young taken from nest to be photographed, Outer Hebrides.

Bottom White-chinned Petrel, Cape Hen or Shoemaker, *Procellaria aequinoctialis*, on nest, photographed at St Georgia.

Right Audubon's Shearwater, *Puffinus lherminieri*, with subspecies, breeds on many tropical islands in all oceans. It is rather smaller than the Manx species, and browner. This one was photographed by flashlight at its rock crevice in the Seychelles.

1629. Then in 1935 a few pairs were discovered breeding on isolated rat-free islets there, now protected and closed to any visitors. Survival of *Pterodroma cahow* hangs in the balance yet: one problem has been to prevent the more powerful tropicbird entering the rock holes where the Cahow breeds. Undoubtedly the Cahow's habit of winter breeding has helped it to survive as at that season there are fewer chances of human interference.

One of the rarest of these *Pterodroma* petrels must be the Taiko, *P. magentae*, once abundant on the Chatham Islands and an important principal source of food in the Stone Age economy of the Maori inhabitants as late as the early nineteenth century, judging by their abundant bones in old middens. Only one specimen existed in museums, taken in the open Pacific in 1867. Dramatically, since 1978, a very few

have been rediscovered in the rough scrub in the rugged part of the main Chatham island, but as yet none has been found breeding.

Still in New Zealand, until 1965 it was not known where Hutton's Shearwater, *Puffinus huttoni*, a southern shearwater closely resembling the Manx Shearwater of European waters, nested. It was thought to be somewhere in the Tasman Sea islands off Australia and New Zealand. In that year it was found nesting in good numbers at altitudes above 1,000 metres in the craggy Seaward Kaikoura Mountains in the South Island. It is so cold here that the bird, on arrival from sea in the spring, may have to dig into snow to find its established burrow and so is about two months later in commencing to breed than its coast-breeding cousin the Fluttering Shearwater, *P. gavia*. Probably because of com-

petition at Fluttering Shearwater burrows on the coast, some of the same species took to breeding on the high Kaikouras, and because of the climate and geographic isolation became the distinct species *P. huttoni* now is; bigger and darker, later in breeding, and wandering farther in winter to Australian coasts, where it does not breed. Here it may encounter two much more migratory *Puffinus* shearwaters, both of which have been closely studied by banding. In particular we have had the pleasure of living for a while on Fisher Island, a tiny islet in the Bass Strait, where since 1948 Dom Serventy has studied the individuals of some 100 pairs. Their migrations follow in the Pacific Ocean a figure-of-eight voyage of several thousand kilometres across the equator similar to that of the Manx Shearwater I studied at Skokholm. But while our Welsh island shearwaters winter as far south as the coast of

The Petrels

Argentina, Serventy's Short-tailed Shearwater, *P. tenuirostris*, circles north to spend its 'winter' in the far North Pacific. It actually penetrates through the Bering Sea to enter the Arctic Ocean where, under the midnight sun, it enjoys the abundant krill plankton close to the pack-ice, among the whales and seals.

Visiting tropical and temperate islands which are covered with forests, it has been strange to us, accustomed to observing albatrosses, shearwaters and smaller petrels breeding on treeless islands of cooler latitudes, to find shearwaters, gadfly and other smaller petrels confidently nesting in burrows they dig under the forest canopy. They are so awkward in getting about on land, with their legs placed so far to the rear of the body when at rest, that we wondered how they could orientate home and also take off – for which they need a clear space for taxiing. These birds have solved the problem by climbing the trees. Using the hooked bill, spread wings and sharp-clawed feet they can almost run up a tree, until they find a clear space at, or near, the top to launch away. Even more astonishing to earthbound man, on returning from the sea the forest-nesting petrels fly unerringly direct to the spot in the canopy above their individual burrow, and flutter vertically down to it. In effect they make a crash landing. In doing so they tumble from branch to branch and occasionally strangle themselves if the neck becomes wedged immovably in a fork; but, as we have seen, when this happens the bird usually manages to use its claws and wings to lift its head clear.

Storm Petrels

There are about 20 species scattered over all oceans of the world, some highly migratory, like the British Storm Petrel, which we studied in those early island days at Skokholm. This revealing study has been continued by other observers up to date, and many thousands have been banded there and at other island colonies in the British and Faeroe Islands. Our Skokholm bird makes an astonishing winter journey across the equator as far as the coasts of the Cape of Good Hope, where we have watched a flock when visiting that noble headland in recent years. Other storm petrels are sedentary within a few hundred kilometres of home. All have the same pattern of breeding described for the large petrels, but much briefer incubation (average 40–50 days) and fledging (60 days) periods. There is usually a four to six year period of adolescence, when the storm petrel may visit coasts and islands at night far from home, as if exploring to establish a new colony – and this sometimes happens.

Hardiest of all is Wilson's Storm Petrel, *Oceanites oceanicus*, nesting along the Antarctic coast where it is often obliged to dig through snow to reach its burrow, which may subsequently be blocked again by a spring or autumn blizzard. Many an egg, chick, even an adult, is entombed in this way, and must die. Yet it is one of the most numerous of seabirds, and a great traveller, flying north to winter in the tropical Indian and Pacific Oceans, and regularly reaching the east coast of North America.

Left Manx Shearwater, *Puffinus puffinus*. So-called from its first naming on the Calf islet off the coast of the Isle of Man. It abounds on certain rat-free islands off the west coast of Britain, the Faeroes, Azores and Madeira, wintering as far south as the coast of Argentina. A few breed on mountain-tops – this picture was taken by flashlight at about 600 metres on the rocky crags of the Hebridean island of Rhum. Tell-tale plots of greener vegetation mark the entrances to their burrows here, as a result of their rich guano, squirted on entering or leaving their hidden nest.

Above Wilson's Storm Petrel, *Oceanites oceanicus*. Although relatively tiny, this is the hardiest small bird in the world, nesting in the snow and ice-troubled screes of Antarctica, where after summer blizzards it frequently has to dig through snow to reach its burrow. In spite of severe weather hazards, it remains one of the most common birds at sea, making a long migration north of the equator to 'winter' in the northern summer. The long legs trail behind the tail in flight, but in feeding the yellow-webbed feet are used to patter over the water – not so much to walk on the surface, as to prevent submergence by bouncing off it.

Right Millions of Sooty Shearwaters, *Puffinus griseus*, inhabit the southern Pacific in the antipodean summer, nesting in burrows which they dig on small islands off New Zealand (three million pairs on the Snares), Tasmania, the Falklands and Chile. In the southern autumn they make a long migration across the equator to enjoy the northern summer as far north as temperate coasts off North America, Japan and the North Atlantic.

Below British Storm Petrel, *Hydrobates pelagicus*, at mouth of burrow, Skomer Island, Wales.

Diving Petrels

These are true petrels but chubby and small, and by an interesting convergent evolution they have occupied in the southern hemisphere the ecological niche of the auks of the northern oceans. Like them, for a while they are flightless at sea while moulting. This is not important, since they obtain their plankton food by diving. They have a distensible pouch in which to store food to carry to the single chick hidden in a deep burrow out of reach of predators – by night. They fly rather laboriously, like bumble bees. Five species, no larger than storm petrels, breed on islands of the sub-Antarctic and the Humboldt current.

CHAPTER 4
Cormorants, Gannets, Boobies and others

The considerable seabird order known as Pelecaniformes contains six families, comprising 7 true species of pelicans, about 29 cormorants, 3 gannets – which prefer cold oceans for breeding, 6 related species of boobies, which are tropical, 5 frigatebirds and 3 tropicbirds or bos'n birds. There are also two darter or anhinga species which, like the pelicans, are more freshwater and estuarine than sea-going. All are powerful swimmers and divers, except the frigatebirds or 'man-of-war' birds, which, strangely, although often seen far from land, prefer not to get their plumage wet!

Frigatebirds

Like the swifts above the land, the frigatebirds are the most aerial of birds above the sea, with short legs adapted for clinging but not for walking. They are highly specialised, with long narrow pointed wings (about 2.4m wingspan) which have a greater surface area in relation to body weight than that of any other species. The bird can obtain an 'honest' living by capturing flying fish on the wing and snatching up squid and other fish, and fish waste, from the surface of the water; but the alternative name of 'man-of-war' bird derives from its best-known image of piratical harrying of other birds which are carrying fish food. It seems able to recognise, probably from the more laboured flight, those which have full crops, although it has been seen to pursue and eventually seize by the tail a booby reluctant to throw up what little it had in its crop. The frigatebird scoops the food up before it reaches the water, by a swift downward swoop.

The nest is usually built at the top of a low tree, of material snatched from the ground or a bush during the graceful flight, which includes hovering as necessary and in preparation for alighting at the nest, or when about to roost. The plain-looking female is courted and mated by one of the several males which have tried to win her favours by inflating the crimson balloon of the throat pouch, two or three displaying in a group as she flies and hovers above, making her selection. Once paired, the male helps in nest-making by stealing sticks from other nests or wherever this

Above This Magnificent Frigatebird, *Fregata magnificens* – a female, distinguishable by her white belly and black throat band, soars off the Kicker Rocks, Galapagos. The most aerial of seabirds, frigatebirds never voluntarily alight on the water, but obtain their fish food by snatching it from the surface, catching flying fish on the wing, and by forcing boobies and other seabirds to disgorge the contents of their crop by harrying them aerially, like the skuas do.

Right A male Great Frigatebird, *F. minor*, inflates his scarlet throat pouch to attract his mate to return to the single white egg on the flimsy stick nest – or to warn off strangers; other hungry frigatebirds may cannibalise an unguarded egg, or young hatchling, by a swift snatch from the air.

Cormorants, Gannets, Boobies and Others

The North Atlantic Gannet, *Sula bassana,* is a success story, ever since it was protected after centuries of slaughter for food at its European and Canadian colonies, which have today increased to a total of around 200,000 breeding pairs. The cool windy seas provide a more reliable source of surface-swimming fish than the calmer tropics, enabling the gannet to rear one chick efficiently where the boobies, laying two or three eggs, have less success.

furniture, generally in short supply, can be seized in hovering flight. Meanwhile the female guards the nest in preparation for laying the single white egg. As soon as this appears he takes over incubation while she, having fasted during this long courtship and guard period, flies away to feed at sea for up to ten days. The same kind of shared incubation as in the petrels follows, but seems a good deal more haphazard, with other frigatebirds flying past, ready if hungry enough to snatch up an unguarded egg or young chick. This does happen, especially when, as mentioned earlier, fish food at sea in the tropical belt is scarce. The partner may be so late returning to relieve the sitting bird that the latter will leave the nest, in which case the egg or chick, as well as the nest, stick for stick, will be carried off by neighbours. Add to this hazard the likelihood of the egg or chick falling out of the nest during the excited wing-waving movements of the parents, and it seems a miracle that the frigatebird maintains its numbers as it does. When about a month old the downy chick is able to cling with its strong claws and prehensile toes, and will stab at unwelcome intruders with its hooked bill. But it is dependent on food supplied by the adults for long after it has left the nest. Even at three or four months old it hangs around supplicating for food at every passing adult. The male Magnificent Frigatebird, *Fregata magnificens,* in the West Indies gives up feeding his child at this stage, leaving the responsibility to his harassed mate. She has to feed herself before she can feed the fledgling, which as a result has its meal at much longer intervals, perhaps of several days, depending on the availability of food. This means that she is exhausted by the time the grown chick is independent (around six to eight months of age). She is quite unprepared to breed again without a long recuperative holiday. In the meantime the male has recovered; he returns to the breeding site where, in the absence of his late partner, he joins other mature males in their startling display groups of 'crimson blossoming' at the tops of the nesting scrub. A.W. Diamond (1972) counted an excess of juvenile females in his study of frigatebirds, which fits the case if the male breeds more often than the female.

Gannets and Boobies

Sula is an old Norse name for the North Atlantic Gannet, *Sula bassana*, given by the great Scandinavian naturalist Linnaeus in his 1758 arrangement of scientific names; and it has persisted for all seven species of these spectacular plunge-diving oceanic birds. They are specialised for hitting the water at considerable speed: the nostrils are externally closed (breathing is by air passages at each side within the bill); air sacs under the feathers of the throat and breast cushion the impact; and the wings are trailed behind the tail to reduce resistance as the bird enters the water. The dive is for the purpose of gaining enough speed to capture, in the bill, fish seen while in the air, and not (as some suppose) to spear the fish. That method is used by the darter – which then has the tricky problem of shaking its bill free of the impaled fish, without losing it.

Gannets, boobies and cormorants have no naked brood patch, but when about to incubate they place the large webbed feet carefully on top of the egg or eggs, then sink down with the breast feathers covering both the eggs and feet. Their four toes are connected by webbing with numerous blood vessels which produce the body heat necessary for incubation. The longest (middle) toe has a useful toothcomb for preening, in the form of a serrated claw.

Boobies lay two eggs, but rarely hatch more than one chick, perhaps because of the erratic fish food supply,

Below The Blue-footed Booby, *Sula nebouxii*, comically calls attention to the vivid blueness of its big webbed feet by lifting them high during display, and alternately cocking the tail. The naked skin on face and throat is dark blue. The female is larger than her partner and, due to the larger dark pupil contrasting with the yellow iris, gives the illusion of a larger eye than that of the male. It is numerous on the Galapagos and adjacent tropical coasts.

Right This is the largest of the six tropical gannets known as boobies. The Masked or Blue-faced Booby, *S. dactylatra*, with wide tropical distribution, delights the eye with its dazzling white plumage set off by the dark mask of the face and tail.

Below left The mated pair conduct elaborate display – as with all gannets – the female loudly trumpeting, but the male answers with a rather feeble whistle.

frequently pirated from them by the frigatebirds of their tropical home. On the other hand gannets lay only one egg, but if given a second one experimentally are capable of raising both resulting chicks; these hatch at midsummer when the shoaling mackerel, herring, garfish and other surface-swimming fish which they feed on are abundant in the cool seas of temperate latitudes. The three species of gannet are very alike in appearance and habits; golden head and neck above vivid hard-white bodies; differing only in the amount of black visible in the tail and wing-secondaries. In their packed colonies each nest is just out of reach of the neighbour's watchful bill, which will strike at any bird trying to walk between. The nest is built up of seaweed collected at sea, and sometimes grass plucked from a cliff, the whole

consolidated with guano as the season proceeds. The pair bond is strong, maintained by alternate brooding and guard duty at the nest, and much display and guttural calling as fully described in several monographs on the gannet, most recently by Bryan Nelson (1978). Although a splendid flying machine once launched, the gannet is a relatively heavy bird and needs either a strong wind or a clear space to taxi into flight. In attempting to leave the gannetry in calm weather it assumes a somewhat comical pose, bill skypointing to keep clear of neighbours as it prepares to jump into the air; but if it fails it thrashes downhill through the other nests, receiving a thorough drubbing from the owners until it is airborne. Those which have nests at the cliff-edge have the advantage here.

Incubation takes 42–46 days. The chick is hatched almost

Above Breeding colony of North Atlantic Gannets, *Sula bassana*, Grassholm Island, Pembrokeshire.

Right Like so many Galapagos birds the Red-footed Booby, *Sula sula*, is extraordinarily tame, allowing a close approach. This adult is the all brown phase. About five per cent of breeding birds resemble the Masked Booby, with varying amounts of pied plumage, but the red feet are distinctive. Graceful in flight, it inhabits islands in all tropical oceans, plunge-diving for its fish food.

Right Because of its very long neck the darter or anhinga is popularly known as the snake-bird. It is a specialised cousin of the cormorants, fishing usually in shallow, tropical lagoons, lakes and rivers. There is no hook to the tip of the bill as in cormorants; in effect the sharp-pointed bill is a spear operated by the trigger of the coiled neck and impaling its prey, which is then tossed into the air with a violent shake of the head to free the bill and deftly caught and swallowed. When the fish is large, its progress down the long neck proceeds as a considerable bulge! This is the African Anhinga, *Anhinga melanogaster*, photographed at Lake Naivasha, Kenya.

naked, but soon grows a white down preliminary to a 'pepper-and-salt' plumage (as we called it when studying and banding thousands of young North Atlantic Gannets at Grassholm, an islet a dozen kilometres west beyond Skokholm). This plumage is dark brown with white specklings at the ends of the feathers, and in this dress they are very fat when ready to leave the gannetry at about 13 weeks. They tumble into the wind down to the sea, quite unable to sustain flight until they have thinned down. But they can dive, and eventually autumn winds will lift them on their dispersal migration. Typical of those long-lived seabirds already described, these juveniles will journey on the traditional off-season voyage of their species, and remain abroad for two years or more. Some will return at three years, but if so will seldom achieve a mate and territory until in mature plumage in their fifth year.

From being extensively hunted during past centuries by man, who collected the fat young 'squabs' in the autumn, today gannets are strictly protected in their main breeding centres, and have increased steadily. Nelson quotes world population in breeding pairs as follows: North Atlantic *S. bassana* 213,000; Australasian *S. serrator* 35,843; Cape or South African *S. capensis* probably 170,000 (this species is exploited for its guano).

Cormorants

Eric's photographs nicely illustrate the extreme contrast between the Flightless Cormorant unique to the Galapagos Islands at the equator, and the very handsome Antarctic or Blue-eyed Cormorant, *Phalacrocorax atriceps*, which nests 'mid snow and ice' from South Georgia southwards along the islands of the Antarctic Peninsula. Like the penguins with which it consorts amid the pack-ice, and often nesting on rocky headlands under glaciated mountains, it finds abundant summer feeding or krill and associated larger fish. It can dive to at least 25m. These hardy cormorants seemed to be rather laboured in flight, and sluggish and indifferent when we photographed their breeding groups. Apparently they migrate very little so long as they can find open water within easy flying distance of their favourite roost.

Cormorants in general are stay-at-home, and as a consequence have evolved into at least 29 species, not counting subspecies, in their own *Phalacrocorax* genus. Among the numerous islands of New Zealand, there are some 14 species (listed in *The New Guide to the Birds of New Zealand*), a few doubtfully valid perhaps, differing but slightly from the cormorant resident on the next archipelago. Thus each of the outlying islands of the Chathams, Pitt Island, Bounty,

Left The world's only flightless cormorant, *Nannopterum harrisi* is found only on the two main islands of Isabela and Fernandina lying close together in the Galapagos Islands. Here pictured in peaceful co-existence with the seaweed-eating marine iguana. Wings were of little advantage to it in this equatorial solitude, before the advent of man. The flight muscles are rudimentary; the stumpy wings serve mostly as ventilators to cool the body on a hot day, as they are extended to dry off after swimming. Only the feet are used for propulsion.

Above A scene at a breeding colony of the Blue-eyed Cormorant, *Phalacrocorax atriceps*, at Port Lochroy, Antarctica, close to the southern limit of this hardiest of all cormorants. A substantial cup-nest is built up clear of meltwater, usually where avalanches are not likely to strike on open headlands and cliff shelves. This picture was taken in February, with the young well grown. So long as these birds can find enough open water to dive for their fish prey, even in winter, they do not migrate. The eye-ring and the naked skin around the eye are bright blue, the bill brown with a yellow wattle above the upper mandible.

Cormorants, Gannets, Boobies and Others

The handsome Pied Cormorant, *Phalacrocorax varius*, is found numerously on all coasts of Australia and New Zealand, nesting in trees on sea cliffs or beside freshwater lakes near the sea.

Auckland, Campbell, and Macquarie have their special cormorant (usually known as a shag in New Zealand). Quite bewildering to the visitor at first, but an excellent place to conduct comparative studies of the ecology of these striking birds so widely distributed elsewhere in the world. Studying colonies of the Pied Cormorant, *P. varius*, near my home in Auckland has been an unexpected delight. Some individuals wounded by flying into high tension wires were rescued and nursed until able to fly. Although released in the tidal river where they were breeding, they returned to be fed, and later brought their children to share the fish handout they were still being given. After feeding they liked to play games, and would pick up leaves and twigs both in the water and when we offered them. A garland of flowers amused them. They would enjoy a 'tug-of-war' with these toys, while the mature cormorants would make incipient nests on the feeding platform. Siblings showed great affection for each other, twining necks as they sat together, especially if they had enjoyed a squawking argument briefly earlier. Two badly damaged waifs, fallen from separate nests, when nursed together became inseparable until they grew their mature plumage after a year. In the Pied Cormorant this is striking: iridescent green-black back, snow-white underparts, bright blue eye-shadow above golden-yellow bare patch below the eye, the iris sea-green. We noticed that each selected its special perch on the platform each time it came back from the sea, and warned off any other (save its special friend). At night each cormorant flies home to roost on its own few inches of tree-branch or rock throughout the year. Gannets, boobies, cormorants, and frigatebirds are all known to sleep heavily at night at home in their crowded colonies. Cormorants are primarily coastal feeders rather than oceanic, but several species live inland by lakes and rivers.

In preparation for breeding, all cormorants acquire brighter facial colours and some develop head plumes and crests by moulting the winter plumage. Soon after shared incubation of the two to five eggs begins, the colours fade and the plumes disappear. The eggs hatch within one month; the chicks are black and naked at first, but are tenderly cared for and fed on regurgitated fish which they take by groping head first into

the parental gullet. In hot dry weather parents bring water to thirsty nestlings, and will shade them with extended wings.

Our Pied Shags, like all the genus, swam under water with closed wings, the stream-lined body paddled along by alternate strokes of the broad webbed feet as they leisurely searched for food. We noticed they would peer under or turn over stones. On sighting a fish the pursuit changed to rapid motion, jerking the body forward with both feet shoving together. Cormorants do not plunge-dive from the air; usually they slide under from the surface, with sometimes a half-somersault head first. Some species will join forces, like pelicans, to round up a shoal of fish at the surface, those birds àt the rear of the formation flying ahead to become the spearhead devouring the fish, in a revolving sequence. On returning to the land after feeding, cormorants stand with wings outstretched for minutes at a time. They are commonly supposed to be drying their wings which are, it is alleged, not waterproof; but it seems to some observers that by adopting this attitude the cormorant is also probably assisting the digestion of its last meal (it often swallows very large flatfish!) by relieving the pressure of the closed wings on the full crop.

Tropicbirds

It is pleasant to meet these svelte pale birds sometimes far out at sea, perhaps 1,000km from land, in the generally rather birdless tropical doldrums. They are at once identified by their extremely long central tail-feathers, blood-red in the Red-tailed Tropicbird, *Phaethon rubricauda*; white in the Red-billed, *P. aethereus*, and the smaller White-tailed Tropicbird, *P. lepturus*.

The birds normally feed on squid and other fish which rise to the surface at night; but will follow a ship for quite long periods in the open sea, when they are seen to plunge-dive, disappearing briefly, rising buoyantly again, and swimming with long tail cocked high before taking off. They freely perch on a ship's superstructure, which habit, and the long tail, has earned the alternative names of bos'n (boatswain) and marlinspike bird. As in frigatebirds the legs are short and ill-

Far left Inland and river cormorants tend to have longer tails than ocean-going species. Longest of all is that of the Reed Cormorant, *Halietor africanus*, photographed at Lake Naivasha, Kenya.

Left The Pelagic Cormorant, *Phalacrocorax pelagicus*, smaller than the more abundant Brandt's Cormorant, as befits its name, wanders all northern Pacific coasts, including those of Alaska, Japan and China; Brandt's is confined to the Pacific coast of North America.

Above The very large King or Rock Cormorant, *P. albiventor*, breeds in large colonies on rocky shores in the Falkland Islands, and north to about 44° S along the east coast of Argentina, building a substantial cup-nest which the owners renew annually.

adapted for walking. The tropicbird flies direct to alight at its nesting hole in steep sea-cliffs and on precipices of volcanic tropical islands, where launching into the air involves little walking. But where there are no suitable cliffs the Red-tail may nest under bushes (Hawaiian atolls), and the White-tail in a fork or hole of a tree, occasionally some distance inland (Christmas Island, Indian Ocean).

An established pair remain faithful down the years to the nest site where they rear their single chick in shared duties: incubation lasts about 35 days. The chick remains up to 100 days, safe in its nest hole or cover, fed at somewhat irregular intervals but growing very fat, and at last heavier than the adult. In the final week the parents abandon it, and it undergoes a fast while its wings are exercised and strengthened for its lone flight into the wide ocean. Most of its life is spent solitarily at sea. The significance of the long tail is obvious when and if you are fortunate to watch the nuptial aerial display of a pair near the breeding ground. There is much hovering and mutual opening and dipping of the tail-streamers, and movement of the webbed feet. Harsh cries accompany these manoeuvres, and excited neighbours in the same colony may fly in to join the performers. Later, during copulation and incubation at the nest, the tail-streamers become bedraggled and often broken.

Far left Yellow feet assist to identify this Spotted Cormorant or Shag, *Phalacrocorax punctatus*, in dull late-autumn plumage. In full spring dress it assumes a double crest, bright blue throat patch, and striped and spotted neck-line and back. It is confined to New Zealand coasts, breeding on rocky islets.

Left Note that these Stewart Island Shags, *P. carunculatus*, have pink feet, otherwise they could be mistaken at a distance for the smaller Pied Shag in its predominant pied phase, which, however, has a white alar bar on the wing. In this photograph, taken at Stewart Island, the dark or bronze phase is also present; mated pairs may be of either phase, or mixed. Nests on flat rock ledges and stacks as far north as the Otago Peninsula, where local birds are larger and heavier. Typical of some other New Zealand cormorants, this shag seems to be evolving into subspecies rapidly.

Below Cormorants are found world-wide, some three dozen species scattered along all shores, and some inhabit inland lakes. This pair, an adult and a juvenile in moult at the end of the breeding season, are difficult to identify of the several *Phalacrocorax* species with pink legs and facial wattle (this shrinks after nesting). But from the wide black neck band in the adult they are evidently the Campbell Island Cormorant, *P. campbelli*, peculiar to the Campbell Islands south of New Zealand, which we visited in 1981.

Preceding page The White-necked Cormorant, *P. lucidus*, is as large as the cosmopolitan Common Cormorant, *P. carbo*, of which it seems to be a recent local offshoot. It is identifiable by the white of the chin extending to the breast and assumes the same white thigh-patch in breeding plumage. Confined to the southern half of Africa, both on the coast and inland waters.

Above The white-throated Australian form of the Little Shag, *Phalacrocorax melanoleucus*, sometimes confused with the Pied Cormorant, *P. varius*.

Odd Seabirds

Somewhere in the classification of seabirds by their structural affinities, the taxonomists have placed two families we must briefly consider here. Both are uncertainly related to the gulls and auks of our next chapters.

Visitors to the great rookeries of the penguins of the sub-Antarctic islands and shores will find a remarkable all-white bird about the size of a bantam hen strolling about tamely, the only seabird – if indeed it is one – to have unwebbed feet. The sheathbill (Chionididae) is the world's smartest scavenger, impudently darting on foot to interrupt penguins or cormorants in the act of feeding their chicks. When the parent turns to face the unwelcome visitor, mouth opened to squawk defiance, the sheathbill nimbly seizes the regurgitated food. But nothing comes amiss; it will snatch at an egg or chick incautiously exposed by a brooding parent, and even the giant petrel is not exempt from this piracy. A pair of sheathbills will combine to raid in this way, one distracting the bird on the nest while the other snatches on the 'blind' side. At other seasons it feeds on carrion, seal faeces and placenta, seaweed and intertidal creatures. The two species of sheathbill are geographically isolated and differ mainly in the colour of bill. As parents themselves sheathbills are devoted to their eggs and chicks, two or three being raised in a nest of debris well hidden under boulders. They defend their

Bottom The European Shag, *P. aristotelis*, is strictly marine. In the breeding season, which starts sometimes in midwinter, the adult develops an upstanding crest and a metallic blue-green sheen to its totally dark plumage.

Below Common Cormorant, *Phalacrocorax carbo*, an Orkney Islands colony.

Below Tropicbirds are essentially oceanic, diving for their squid food chiefly at night. Their small feet are ill-adapted for walking; they fly direct to their nest in a cliff crevice, occasionally in the crutch of a tree, The White-tailed, *Phaeton lepturus*, depicted here was photographed at the Seychelles, but may be seen in all tropical oceans.

nesting and feeding territories against other sheathbills, using the sharp spurs on their carpal (wing) joints much as bantam cocks do their leg-spurs. This results in a thin distribution of a few pairs to each colony of several hundred penguins, and evidently their parasitism has a healthy effect, disposing of the inefficient or weak and ensuring the survival of the fittest.

Phalaropes are small, dainty, beautiful long-necked species, one of the numerous wader family, some of which make long-distance migrations annually to and from Arctic and sub-Arctic lands. There are three species; the Wilson's Phalarope, *Phalaropus tricolor*, is more terrestrial in habits and appears to migrate chiefly overland. The Grey, *Phalaropus fulicarius*, and the Red-necked, *Phalaropus lobatus*, are unique in that, nesting in the High Arctic by freshwater pools and saltwater estuaries, they spend the winter at sea in the southern hemisphere. They are specially adapted to life in cool ocean waters, having thick plumage with a dense underdown for warmth during continuous swimming. Their feet are partially webbed or lobed along each toe, rather like the grebe's feet, enabling the downward 'propulsion' stroke to provide full pressure, while on the upward stroke the lobes collapse to offer less resistance. This also assists their normal feeding behaviour, a rapid paddling and pirouetting at the surface which draws towards them their planktonic food, eagerly snapped up with fast-dipping bill. Phalaropes fly at

Above A Pacific and Indian Ocean species, the Red-billed Tropicbird, *P. aethereus*, nesting gregariously in holes in the lava rock, is seen here gliding with typical grace near the Galapagos Islands. The two long central tail-feathers are for aerial display when breeding, and may become abraded and broken during shared incubation of the single egg in a rock crevice.

great speed, forming large parties to move from one source of planktonic food to another. We have seen thousands in some of the Alaskan fiords at midsummer, among the auks and whales of that region, feeding where the chill water upwells at the base of glaciers. Some of these phalaropes were perhaps immatures, returned from wintering in the southern summer along the Chilean coast and the cool food-rich waters of the Humboldt current, but many were adult females, judging from their bright colour.

The female phalarope is more brilliantly coloured than the male, as befits her reversed role: she initiates courtship, encouraging the duller-coloured male to mate – usually in shallow water. Afterwards he selects a suitable nest-site, made by breast-rotating in the tundra vegetation. But as soon as she has laid her four richly spotted and blotched eggs, she flies away. She may flirt with a second male, mate and lay another clutch, then fly off, this time for good, making an early migration south or leaving to feed at a glacier front. Each abandoned husband redirects his pair-bond to the eggs, and hatches them alone. The chicks are precocious, running about and finding food themselves soon after birth. Father guards them until they are quite independent at three weeks of age.

Of the numerous wading birds in the world, two of the three phalaropes are uniquely adapted for ocean-going and feeding at sea. With their curiously lobed webbed feet they stir up surface plankton as they pirouette while swimming, snapping up this food with dipping bill. Both Grey **above right** *Phalaropus fulicarius* (pictured here in Iceland), and **right** Red-necked *P. lobatus* (in Shetland) breed in the high Arctic, and migrate across the equator to winter in plankton-rich seas. The Grey reaches farthest south, to feed in the chill currents off Chile and South Africa. These beautiful and dainty little waders fly at great speed, living their intensely active lives far from the haunts of man.

CHAPTER 5
Skuas, Gulls and Terns

Taxonomists have yet to agree fully on the number of *Catharacta* skua species; opinions range from two species to four. Whatever the final decision the *Catharacta* assemblage, and its cousins, the three *Stercorarius* species, which are referred to as jaegers in North America, are placed in the order of Charadriiformes. This large order includes gulls, terns and shorebirds (including waders), which have webbed feet, lay two or more well-marked and coloured eggs, producing at hatching well-developed down-covered young.

In their piratical and scavenging habits at sea and at their breeding grounds skuas and jaegers are even more aggressive than the frigatebirds (page 96), with the further advantage of being as nimble on foot as a gull or tern – or sheathbill. They are extremely bold and will 'dive-bomb' the trespasser near their nest, striking the human head with

Above Great Skua, *Catharacta skua*, attacking intruder on breeding territory, Shetlands.

Right This McCormick's Skua, *Catharacta maccormicki*, seen flying off Cape Hallet in the Ross Sea, is parasitic in summer on penguin colonies, each breeding pair 'guarding' and exploiting a section of a large (usually Adelie) rookery. For the first few years of their lives juvenile McCormick's Skuas are more migratory than *C. skua*, and birds ringed in Antarctica have reached Greenland and Japan.

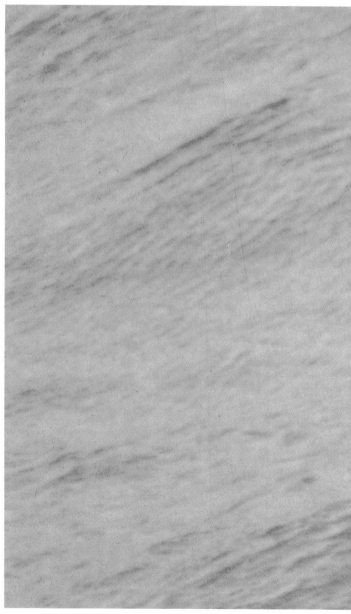

hard blows of wings or feet, occasionally drawing blood with the powerful hooked bill. They follow ships at sea; and at their breeding grounds stand about near the camps or huts of visitors, ready to snatch up waste food. There are some grim accounts of the South Polar Skua, *Catharacta maccormicki*, attacking men skinning seals on the ice, and even on the deck of a ship. The sight of blood seems to rouse a hungry skua to attack the source. Thus skuas attend the birth of seals on beach or ice and may damage the emergent pup before its dam has had time to turn around and protect it. They are of course eager to feast on the afterbirth, which is quickly cleared up. They may also kill a baby seal if its mother is away by gouging out the eyes first. According to some experts seals are safe from this menace if they lie face down. He tested this theory by lying down himself on the deck

where a seal had been flensed during the period his whaling ship was temporarily trapped in pack-ice. They attacked him only when he lay face uppermost. These South Polar Skuas were so determined that they drove the ship's cat to cover, and forced the crew to skin the seals they had caught under a canvas shelter.

During our visits to Antarctica and Arctic shores we received from angry skuas no more harm than a blow on the head – well-protected by a thick sheepskin cap. The Great Skua, *Catharacta skua*, of the sub-Arctic (Bear Island, Iceland, northern isles of Scotland) is very similar to the dark phase of the South Polar Skua. Lately it has been proved by banding recovery that the South Polar Skua migrates into the higher latitudes of the Pacific and Atlantic Oceans, perhaps also the Indian Ocean. One South Polar Skua, banded as a nestling in

the Antarctic (January 1975), was shot six months later in Greenland. Specimens have also been collected off California and Newfoundland. It has recently been suggested that the *Catharacta* group originated in the southern hemisphere and split into several distinct forms, one of which followed the migrating shearwaters and petrels north and remained there to colonise sub-Arctic islands and shores.

It has been remarked that the South Polar Skua holds the record for being the first free-flying bird to reach the South Pole. Just one record so far, but it has often been seen hundreds of kilometres inland flying over the lifeless Antarctic ice-cap.

Although skuas prey opportunistically on the eggs and chicks of penguins, gulls, terns and other seabirds nesting in dense colonies within their own breeding range, they are not necessarily dependent on this source for food to supply to their own chicks. At the large Adelie Penguin colonies on Ross Island, E.C. Young over five summers worked out the territorial requirements of the attendant South Polar Skuas. No established pair in control of a part of the penguin rookery could obtain enough food without feeding at sea for at least a part of the four month breeding season. Nesting territories within penguin rookeries were fiercely defended by violent display, and by attacking other skua neighbours and interlopers. Year after year the same territorial boundaries were maintained by the same pairs. But if by natural accident one or both partners failed to return, the established neighbours were inhibited from claiming the vacant territory because they 'remembered' being attacked if they dared to cross the boundary. In any case, before they could explore in that

Left The large Great Skua, *Catharacta skua*, seen here off the Antarctic Peninsula feeding with Kelp Gulls on refuse thrown from our ship, is identical in the field with the Great Skua breeding in Iceland, the Faeroes and northern Scotland (we also found it nesting farther north, on Bear Island). It is extremely rapacious, aggressively attacking sick or wounded birds or seals, snatching at unguarded eggs or chicks, scavenging afterbirth and carcasses.

Below Long-tailed Skua, *Stercorarius longicaudus*, incubating eggs, Iceland.

direction, replacement pairs, always scouting by air at a respectful distance, would within a few days or hours drop into and defend the vacant plot. These replacement pairs or individuals came from a club of unattached, chiefly inexperienced young or lately bereaved adults, which assembles on the edge of the colony of most colonial-nesting birds. Here they indulge in idle preening, mild sweethearting and other social activities, an assembly essentially derived from the 'compulsion to love', or in more vulgar terms, the overwhelming desire to mate, but which is inhibited by lack of the space necessary for successful reproduction, i.e. a territory and home in which the pair-bonds may be consolidated by display and coition in comparative freedom.

It is the same story for all territorial species of birds and other animals, already remarked in this book, that as a result of established pairs recognising, through conflict at the boundaries of their territory, the limits of their property, the size and shape of that territory tend to remain the same from year to year, even when occupied by new individuals.

Having watched the smaller skuas (jaeger is a more appropriate name for these swift long-tailed pirates) in their breeding grounds, from the Shetlands north to the Arctic tundra, it was pleasant to meet some of them in their winter wanderings: for instance in sight of my home by the Hauaraki Gulf in New Zealand, the Arctic Jaeger, *Stercorarius parasiticus*, is common, often pursuing local gulls and terns to force them to drop a load of fish during their nesting season, November to February. These jaegers are mostly young birds hatched in the northern summer about six months earlier and in no hurry to return north. In fact they may spend a whole year with us before they return north. These immatures lack the long centre tail-feathers of the breeding dress of jaegers, but their dark plumage and piratical habits make them easy to identify.

All three jaeger species breed only in the north, but winter in the southern oceans. At home on their tundra nesting grounds these swift-flying graceful jaegers prey much on the eggs and chicks of the numerous wading birds which throng the Arctic wetlands and moors briefly at midsummer. When these depart, the jaegers fatten on the summer increase of small rodents, especially the ground-burrowing lemmings. Early in the autumn they join the migrating gulls and terns, which they will harry as they move south towards the equator, and beyond. The jaegers have banished winter from their lives.

Above Northern Great Skua standing over nest in Shetlands.

Right A light phase Arctic Skua, *Stercorarius parasiticus*, returns to its nest in the Orkney Isles. Breeding in all high Arctic latitudes south to northern Scotland and the Aleutian Isles, this skua migrates to 'winter' as far south as New Zealand, Tierra del Fuego and South African coasts, harrying concentrations of other seabirds feeding in those fertile seas during the southern summer.

Gulls

We have already mentioned these graceful flying machines, which hover and glide in more leisurely fashion than the skuas, jaegers and frigatebirds, which easily overtake them in piratical pursuit. Gulls are the most conspicuous and best-known seabirds in the world, occupying every shore from the polar ice-caps to the equator. With one odd exception: they are absent from the warmer Polynesian islets of the South Pacific, where their habitat is largely occupied by the Sooty, *Sterna fuscata*, White, *Gygis alba*, and Noddy Terns, *Anous stolidus*.

There are some 45 species of gull (Eric has photographed more than half) but many are inland nesters, visiting salt water only on migration. The majority of these inland gulls wear, in summer, dark brown or black hoods: they are omnivorous, taking fish and aquatic organisms in river and lake, and whatever small life they can find on land, including hawking after insects in the air. Other gulls are more marine, or littoral, finding a living along the shore or within a few kilometres of the land. They will follow ships and fishing vessels to pick up edible waste; and the plough or other farm machines cultivating the soil.

Of the smaller gulls which follow ships, but not to take offal – they seek the small planktonic organisms churned up by the ship's passage – the Kittiwake, *Rissa tridactyla*, is the most ocean-going. It is circumpolar as a northern hemisphere and High Arctic breeder. There is a Red-legged form of the Kittiwake, *Rissa brevirostris*, in the Bering Sea area of the Pacific, generally regarded today as a true species, as

although the Common (Black-legged) Kittiwake nests in the same area and is more abundant, the Red-legged Kittiwake is confined to one or two nesting sites. Moreover they do not interbreed and the Red-legged juvenile has a white tail, but the Black-legged young bird has a black-tipped tail.

Wandering all winter far across the open ocean, the Kittiwake returns to the steep cliffs where it was born, to build its nests in the spring. It selects the narrowest ledges and footholds on which to fix seaweed, grass and other vegetation which it treads into a compact state, soon to be cemented with squirts of guano. In the tiny cup of this precarious nursery one to three eggs are incubated by both partners in turn for rather less than a month. Kittiwakes at home make a delightful study; they are comparatively tame,

provided the observer approaches quietly. Because of the shortage of standing room, the mated pair are obliged to confine their courtship display to waving, nodding of the head, and intimate twining of necks, uttering their 'kitt-i-wake' cries. The mouth is freely opened to exhibit the deep yellow gape and tongue, and there is a kind of choking or gulping motion of the arched neck, as if the bird was about to regurgitate. The male does this at intervals, and feeds the female, who begs for it (see page 31). There is no room for other manoeuvres on the tiny nest. The mated pair, and later the young birds, of necessity sit with breasts facing the cliff, tails extending in space. But nature has provided this gull with strong claws to its webbed feet, with which it clings firmly to the nest-cup when gales threaten to sweep it away.

Left Newly-fledged Kittiwake, *Rissa tridactyla*, at the Farne Isles, showing dark markings of immature plumage absent in the breeding adults.

Below A typical cliff-ledge nesting colony of Kittiwakes in Iceland.

Above The Californian Gull, *Larus californicus*, closely resembles a small Herring Gull with a dark mantle. This picture nicely shows the difference in plumages of the juvenile, adult and sub-adult; the last exhibits the dusky sub-terminal band on the bill, which is never quite lost in the mature bird.

Left Indian Brown-headed Gull, *Larus brunnicephalus*, winter plumage.

Right The Herring Gull, *L. argentatus*, is the most abundantly found gull along the littoral temperate coasts of the North Atlantic, from north-west Europe to Canada and the United States. It has increased enormously as the result of the availability of waste food at rubbish dumps, fish wharves and fishing vessels working close to the coast. It is not truly oceanic, migrating only locally in search of food.

Experiments have shown that when a young Kittiwake, unable to fly, is placed on a pedestal one metre or so above the ground, it will not attempt to leave. The instinct to stay put is a survival habit; young birds which did not do so in nature would fall to their death.

Gulls nesting in more spacious habitats behave differently. When alarmed the chick, if unable to fly, either crouches (if very young) or walks away and hides in the nearest cover. If there is none, it continues to walk away from the intruder, and may fall over a cliff. Its fate then depends on how hard it hits the next object: if it falls into the sea, it at once swims to the nearest point of land and does its best to climb back, encouraged by its distressed parents flying overhead, watchfully uttering the warning cry. Hence it is a mistake, with

serious consequences for the birds, for the observer to walk about in a large gull colony with many nests close together containing growing chicks. Although in the uproar of gull cries the parents are able to recognise the peeping voices of their own disturbed progeny, unless these youngsters get back home in good time they may die from various causes. Herring, *Larus argentatus*, Great, *L. marinus*, and Lesser Black-backed, *L. fuscus*, are merciless if a chick they do not recognise happens to wander into their territory: they will attack it, and unless it runs away fast enough it will be killed – and eaten. We have also seen, rarely, a small chick which, tumbled from its nest by the sudden flight of the brooding adult on the appearance of a human passer-by, struggled for half an hour to get back to its nest over rough terrain. When

at last it approached its parent (brooding two siblings) the adult attacked, killed and ate it – and later fed the semi-digested body by regurgitation to those siblings.

Cannibalism is of course a form of population control. We mention it deliberately here, but it does occur increasingly in the large overcrowded colonies of gulls on many coasts where the human population is concentrated in big cities. The scavenging *Larus* gull species have multiplied dramatically in the present century because of the abundance of waste protein continuously available at rubbish dumps, sewage and meatwork outfalls, fish wharves, and fishing vessels within easy gulls' flight of the coast. This is obvious, even to the most stay-at-home urban dweller, in the number of gulls which flock to be fed in city parks, back gardens and

picnic places. In New Zealand the pretty red-footed and red-billed Silver Gull, *L. novaehollandiae scopulinus*, is often dubbed the 'Picnic Gull' because groups of individuals have become dependent largely on handouts of household scraps. In the same country the large Black-backed or Dominican Gull, *L. dominicanus*, once rare and hunted for food by the Maori, has begun to nest on tall buildings in Auckland and Wellington, convenient for waste food supplied by the inhabitants.

When these scavenger gulls feel the urge to breed, and fly to their traditional sites (usually safe from serious human interference though invariably within range of this man-provided food source), there is often a lack of adequate nesting space for their enlarged numbers. Severe competition for the most desirable sites results in territorial struggles,

Left The Kelp, Dominican or Southern Black-backed Gull, *Larus dominicanus*, inhabits all cool latitudes of southern hemisphere coasts, including the sub-Antarctic islands, but is absent from Polynesia and much of southern Australia. It occupies the southern niche of food and territory comparable with that of the larger Great Black-backed *L. marinus* of the northern hemisphere, being just as predatory and aggressive.

Above Red-billed (Silver) Gulls *L. novaehollandiae*, face the wind as the tide ebbs at Stewart Island.

Below Great Black-backed Gull, *L. marinus*, attending young at nest in Shetland.

Left The Black-headed Gull of
Eurasia, *Larus ridibundus*, is
another success story, greatly
increased in the present century
as a scavenger of waste food at
dumps, urban parks and picnic
areas (where it becomes almost
hand-tame) and following plough
and harrow cultivating the land.
The dark brown hood is moulted
in the autumn and absent in the
first juvenile plumage. A group in
Kew Gardens, London.

Right Mating European Black-
headed Gulls,· *Larus ridibundus*,
Suffolk.

Above The Laughing Gull, *Larus
atricilla*, of eastern North America
has a neck-length grey-black hood
which disappears in the winter,
when it migrates from its Atlantic
nesting grounds south to Brazil;
some cross the Gulf of Panama to
the coast of Ecuador. Note the
black bill and dark-red legs.

Left The Common or Mew Gull, *L.
canus*, is distributed throughout
the temperate northern latitudes,
nesting both inland and close to
the sea, often in association with
terns. Photographed at the nest in
the Shetlands.

Above right A Ring-billed Gull, *L.
delawarensis*, at Bodega Bay,
California. Very like the Mew Gull,
L. canus, with yellow bill and legs,
but marked by the black band on
the bill. An inland breeder in
central USA, migrating to both
coasts in winter.

raiding of each other's nests, and occasional cannibalism.
'Safe' gull nesting colonies are usually on islands or steep
cliffs also occupied by other seabirds, some of the smaller of
which (puffins, guillemots, other auks, terns and waders),
and their eggs and young, seasonally (conveniently) provide
a handy source of food for the enlarged gulleries. Hence man,
who today would protect, by law and inclination, what he
calls the 'inoffensive' species of seabirds, is indirectly re-
sponsible for the great increase of their gull predators. In
many coastal and island sanctuaries set aside for seabirds,
campaigns are now in action to reduce if not eliminate the
'gull scourge'. Conservationists in general love nature, but do
not always accept the way nature adjusts to a situation.

As observed undisturbed at the nest, all gulls are normally
model partners, affectionate and tender in caring for the

133

Left We encountered the ethereal-looking snow-white Ivory Gull, *Pagophila eburnea*, at Spitsbergen, and as far north as our ship could go in the pack-ice in summer. Probably the hardiest gull in the world, it remains close to the ice all the year, following polar bears and sea-mammals for what it may pick up in the way of flesh, carrion and faeces; it also feeds on plankton and insects where available. Note the black bill, feet and eyes in this trio feeding (with a Great Black-backed Gull, *Larus marinus*) on the remains of a bearded seal, freshly killed and partly devoured by a polar bear, which reluctantly left the ice floe as our ship came close.

Right The Western Gull of California and British Columbia, *Larus occidentalis*, resembles our British Lesser Black-backed, *Larus fuscus*, being about the same size, but this western American *Larus* has red legs, a greyer mantle and is non-migratory.

Far right The Glaucous-winged Gull, *L. glaucescens*, pictured at Morris Bay, Washington State, is large, but not as large as the Glaucous Gull, *L. hyperboreus*. Both may meet at winter quarters on the west coast of North America. The Glaucous-winged Gull in adult plumage has a blue-grey mantle like the Herring Gull and nests only on the coasts of the Bering Sea and the Aleutian chain.

young chicks. We have seen a Herring Gull male caress his sitting mate's head, and later rest one foot on her back for long intervals, as if claiming proprietorship – as in effect he was. The cryptically coloured downy chick is nursed continually for the first two weeks of the vulnerable period, one parent remaining on guard while the other is away foraging. When hungry the hatchling pecks towards the conspicuous red spot on the lower mandible of the parent (Herring, Great and Lesser Black-backed, Pacific, *L. pacificus*, Dominican, Western, *L. occidentalis*, and some other *Larus* gulls): this tapping is evidently a 'releaser', inducing the parent to pump food from its crop to its bill where it is held and allowed to trickle into the chick's gaping mouth.

We may note that if a spot of another colour is conspicuous at the tip of a gull's bill, the youngster will aim at this just the same, or at any spot elsewhere about the bill which stands out conspicuously. Thus in the adult Swallow-tailed Gull, the bill is dark green, almost black, with a grey tip. According to Harris (1970) the chick pecks both towards the tip, and at the white patches at the base of the mandibles. This Swallow-tailed Gull is very handsome with its dark hood, huge eyes with crimson eyelids, white breast, bluish back and red feet. With its long forked tail it is tern-like in flight, with slow wing-beats. It is the only nocturnal gull in the world, going

forth at night from its large noisy colonies in the Galapagos to find its squid food. In contrast, the Lava or Dusky Gull, *Larus fuliginosus*, endemic to the Galapagos Is, mostly sooty-grey but with a white eye-ring, is a cheeky scavenger of beaches and human settlements, predates other birds' eggs, and devours newly-hatched marine iguanas. Curiously, it nests solitarily, retreating to a remote lava field to rear its two chicks. Both Galapagos gulls nest at any time of the year, depending on the abundance of marine food.

It has lately been discovered, in a study by J.A. Mills (1973), that there is a surplus of adult females in the breeding population of the New Zealand Silver Gull. As, like all *Larus* gulls, the species is monogamous, this means that the young female has some problem in obtaining a mate, and may have to wait a further year or two because she is not courted by a sexually mature male. Conversely it means that the young male will breed earlier, with a surplus of sexually mature debutantes available.

The larger gulls take up to four years to acquire fully adult plumage, although some will breed at three years. This long period of adolescence explains the presence of mobs of gulls roosting and feeding in urban situations all the year round. City reservoirs, urban lakes, and the roofs of large factories, are popular night roosts with the minimum of disturbance.

Terns

Sea-swallow is a more descriptive name for these graceful long-winged birds. There are 42 species, their distribution covering all oceans and the major inland lakes. Some of the tropical species are more or less sedentary; others, breeding in cold latitudes, are highly migratory. Longest distance traveller in the bird world must be the Arctic Tern, *Sterna paradisaea*. Nesting as far north as there is land around the Arctic Ocean, it yet flies up to 20,000 kilometres (12,420 miles) to 'winter' as far south as there is salt water, at the edge of the pack-ice of the Antarctic continent. Thus it enjoys more sunlight annually than any other living creature on earth. We have been 'dive-bombed' by breeding Arctic Terns at Spitsbergen (repeatedly struck on the head by a pair attacking in sequence!); eighteen months earlier, we identified Arctic Terns fishing and resting amid Antarctic ice floes in the Ross Sea.

Interestingly there is a closely related Antarctic Tern, *Sterna vittata*, breeding on the coast of the Antarctic Peninsula and sub-Antarctic islands. Probably it evolved from migratory Arctic Tern stock which, finding conditions suitable for permanent residence, failed to migrate north in the austral autumn. In breeding plumage the two species can hardly be distinguished in the field; but fortunately for the

birdwatcher in Antarctica in summer the resident tern is in full beauty with rich black cap, while at that season (its 'winter') the visiting Arctic Tern is usually in ragged moult, the forehead and breast white, and the tail-streamers absent.

It is an often remarked fact that the Arctic Tern, on its record transequatorial migration, has rarely been seen to rest on the sea. Like the migrating European Swift, *Apus apus*, over the land, it is almost always in the air; we have never seen it alight at sea, except occasionally when it will rest on a large floating object such as a driftwood log. The same tireless flight has been observed of the Sooty Tern, another oceanic traveller. Although both these terns – and most tern species – feed by snatching up small fish at the surface, they prefer to do so without submerging, rising instantly in flight almost as if afraid to wet their wings. There is good reason for the mature Arctic Tern to hurry south on strong wings. It delays shedding its wing and tail quills until it can rest in the same cool climate of a polar summer it was born in. Some Arctic Terns, born in lower northern latitudes (Scotland, Iceland) may not reach as far south as Antarctica: it is generally true that individuals of a migratory species nesting nearest the poles make the longest migrations (*vide* South Polar Skua and Arctic Jaeger mentioned earlier). In effect, the adult breeders 'leap-frog' on their migration and pass less active birds in order to enjoy a similar climate in the opposite hemisphere. It

Above Great Black-headed Gull, *Larus ichthyaetus*, a very large gull, Bangladesh.

Right The Sooty or Aden Gull, *Larus hemprichi*, common on the East African coast, is a scavenger. This individual was photographed taking offal at the Mombasa fish market, Kenya.

Top The Swallow-tailed Gull, *Creagrus furcatus*, of spectacular appearance is another local Galapagos species, up to 15,000 pairs breeding colonially on certain small islands and cliffs. It is the only nocturnal gull known, hence the very large light-gathering eyes. In flight it is tern-like, with long wings and a long forked tail.

Above The tiny Little Gull, *Larus minutus*, as it appears here in winter plumage at Minsmere, Suffolk. In summer it has a black hood and red bill and legs. Has bred rarely in Britain, but its main nesting grounds are inland waters of temperate Eurasia.

Right The lava-coloured Lava or Dusky Gull, *L. fuliginosus*, is unique to the Galapagos Isles, where it is an opportunistic scavenger of the shore and human precincts. Yet it prefers to nest solitarily, away from man on lonely lava screes.

Below Antarctic Tern, *Sterna vittata*, alighting at nest on South Georgia.

should be noted, however, that terns in general do not assume full breeding dress until two years old, and numbers of one-year-old Arctic Terns may spend their first 'summer' feeding in the cool waters of the Humboldt or Benguela currents before they are sexually mature enough to return to the far north.

Terns in general have a similar breeding regime to the gulls. Shared incubation occupies less than a full month, and the fledging period is somewhat shorter at four to five weeks. Although some terns will fiercely attack an intruder, human or other animal, their colonies are often very large and conspicuous, and could not succeed if they were not sited in places least vulnerable to marauding predators. If repeatedly disturbed at the egg-laying stage, the whole mob of breeding adults may quite suddenly desert an established ternery and move to a new site. This may be too late for the birds to raise broods in the same season, but if the new site is safer than the old, they will return to the new one next year. This behaviour has been noted in Arctic, Common, *S. hirundo*, Sandwich, *S. sandvicensis*, Caspian, *S. caspia*, and other terns which nest colonially.

Like some penguins and pelicans, some terns form crèches where the young, while still unable to fly, are shepherded by adults and can be moved in a mob along a beach for their better survival in bad weather, or against predation. Sooty

Bottom These four Caspian Terns, *Sterna caspia*, were photographed in a muddy estuary in view of Ronald's Auckland home in New Zealand, in March. The breeding season is over, and the adult on the left is losing its black monk's cap, while the three juveniles have not yet acquired more than a darkness around the eye. A cosmopolitan tern breeding in all temperate and semi-temperate lands, except South America.

Below A gathering of White-fronted Terns, *Sterna striata*, resting on the rocky shore at Stewart Island after feeding. Although confined as a breeder to New Zealand, a large number make an unusual latitudinal migration to spend most of their winter along the south-east coast of Australia – where they do not breed. It nests colonially on rock islets, sand dunes and remote pebbly beaches.

Overleaf The White Tern, *Gygis alba*, in flight (over the Seychelles) is fairy-like; but the Fairy Tern proper, *Sterna nereis*, although much the same size, and just as graceful in flight, wears a black cap, and is restricted to nesting on Australian, New Caledonia and northern coasts of New Zealand.

Above Juvenile Gull-billed Tern,
Gelochelidon nilotica, Pakistan.

Tern colonies are often so immense and their crèches so densely packed with young birds that it seems impossible that the parents can find and recognise their chick (usually one only; most terns lay two or three eggs). But somehow it is found by voice recognition, and fed on the fish carried raw in the parental bill. Some observers have recorded that a persistent young tern can successfully beg food from a fish-carrying adult not its real parent.

The charming, delicate-looking Noddy Terns inhabit tropical islands and shores, normally building quite substantial nests of leaves in tall bushes or trees – including mangroves. Although they do not usually stray far from home, they have shown an impressive ability to return home when experimentally released 2,000km (1,200 miles) from their nesting island. Some populations are migratory. Large colonies are very noisy, as they make their displays and dart about in zigzag fashion. At times, as at most tern colonies, a majority will suddenly rise together, silently, high up above the nesting ground: this is known as a 'dread', probably triggered by a sudden louder alarm call the observer may not have heard; it is quickly over and the terns drop rapidly back to their territories with much clamour.

The small White Tern is remarkable in laying its single egg on a bare branch of a tree (occasionally on a rock ridge), yet does not often lose it through bad weather or awkward

Far left The dainty and charming White Tern, *Gygis alba*, lays its single egg and rears its chick apparently precariously on a branch, yet nurses it so assiduously that it rarely topples over, even in a gale. The parent on duty will not easily leave when you approach (giving the impression of tameness; but it is obvious that the adult is instinctively aware of the dangers of leaving). It nests on tropical islands in all oceans; here photographed at the Seychelles.

Left The Whiskered Tern, *Chlidonias hybridus*, is a lover of warm latitudes, here seen at the famous nature Reserve of the Coto Doñana marshes, Spain. Note the short tail of this inland swamp breeder, which is found throughout south-east Europe and across India to Australian swamps; and also in Madagascar and South Africa.

Below White-winged Black Tern, *C. leucopterus*, migrants resting at Lake Nakuru, Kenya. Even smaller than the Little Tern, this mottled sprite is shown here in offseason plumage, far from its central Eurasian breeding marshes. We have seen an occasional individual even in New Zealand.

Left An adult male Common Tern, *Sterna hirundo*, presents his mate with a fish, typical courtship behaviour of many tern species, at a gravel pit colony, Huntingdon, England. It is almost impossible to distinguish this species from the Arctic Tern unless the black tip to the scarlet bill is noticed; it being absent from the latter. It is not such a long-distance traveller; breeding on both sides of the Atlantic, and throughout temperate Eurasia, it is absent from the Pacific side of North America.

Below The Lesser Noddy, *Anous tenuirostris*, builds a substantial nest in bush or tree, in small colonies on the Seychelles and some other Indian Ocean Islands, often in mangroves, convenient to fishing at high tide.

movement of the owners. It is a very beautiful creature, snow white except for the dark bill and eye-ring. On sub-tropical Norfolk Island we found it incubating its egg more safely on the branches of the tall indigenous pine which are fringed with upstanding green branchlets of fine leaves acting as a fence to retain the egg even in a fresh wind tossing the boughs.

Skimmers are not oceanic; they feed by 'ploughing' the smooth water of estuaries and lakes with the longer lower mandible as they fly with open mouth and wings held high – beating above the horizontal. They feed in the twilight of evening and often by moonlight, when their small fish prey are rising to the surface. Without pausing when a fish is trapped, the skimmer snaps the upper mandible shut with a scissors-sharp cutting action, gulps the catch down, and ploughs on again. Small aquatic organisms rise to the line of luminescence left by the furrowing bill; and the skimmer will double back, and dexterously capture these. Favourite nesting sites of the three species are the shingle beds of rivers, which they may share with terns, during the dry season.

Above The Arctic Tern, *Sterna paradisaea*, is the world's longest distance migrant. Those which nest farthest north, on Arctic Ocean coasts, may travel south to winter in the long sunlight of the Antarctic summer; thus enjoying almost perpetual daylight, save for their few weeks of nights passing through the tropics. Moreover, on this flight they are seldom or never seen to alight and rest on the sea; feeding is by snatching or short dives at the surface, the wings never closed.

Above right Lesser Crested Tern, *Sterna bengalensis*, Bangladesh.

Right Adult Sandwich Tern, *Sterna sandvicensis*, feeding young.

CHAPTER 6
The Auks

There are 21 living species of these penguin-like birds, 19 of which live, or have been recorded, in the North Pacific, that oldest of oceans which must have seen their origin and speciation (page 44). They share certain structural affinities with gulls, terns and web-footed wading birds. The considerable differences in the shape of the bills of the auks relate to their mode of capturing their marine food.

The long sharp-pointed bill of the guillemots is adapted to catching and holding a single fish *lengthwise*. The prey is often longer than the bill, so that the tail may protrude beyond the tip – as may be seen when an adult brings in a fish for its single chick on the cliff ledges. It will be noticed that, on first arrival with the fish, the parent does not immediately deliver it to the chick, whether or not it is supplicating with

wheezy cries to be fed. This delay, it has been suggested, is because the tough head, well-down inside the parental crop, is being partly digested by the juices (salivary amylase) – just as pigeons soften grain in preparation for feeding their squab. It is thus easier for the youngster to assimilate when, with a dexterous turnabout in the adult mouth, the fish is presented head-first to the hungry chick. In any case the horny fish head will have been well lubricated by the mucus or saliva in the adult crop, to aid its slippery passage into that of the chick. The Razorbill, *Alca torda*, nesting on slightly less precipitous cliffs and screes, brings home two or three small fish held loosely *across* the closed bill. The huge, spectacularly coloured and vertically flattened bill of the Atlantic Puffin, *Fratercula arctica*, can hold up to 28 little fish (we have

counted this number when a surprised adult dropped them), usually fewer, when carrying food home to the chick born in a deep burrow. This is made possible by the roof of the mouth and the top of the tongue being furnished with short inward-facing spines.

The Little Auk, *Alle alle*, of the High Arctic and several small North Pacific auklets collect even smaller fish and zooplankton, which they store in throat pouches under the tongue to feed to their chicks hidden in holes and under rock-falls. These small auks are not easy to study; like the Black Guillemot, *Cepphus grylle*, they lay their eggs where they are not easily reached by prowling fox or predatory bird. But it does mean that, in comparative safety here, the young bird need be in no hurry to get away to sea. But the guillemots and

The Auks

Preceding page The chubby body of the Black Guillemot, *Cepphus grylle*, back view in Spitsbergen waters, displays the white patches of its black summer dress. Here it lays two eggs well hidden from Arctic foxes deep under boulders close to the sea. It breeds on all high Arctic and North Atlantic coasts south of the British Isles and the coast of Maine in New England. The Pacific representative is the very similar Pigeon Guillemot, *C. columba*.

Above Razorbills, *Alca torda*, at Skomer Island, Wales.

Right Razorbills and guillemots resting on the sea under the cliffs at Bardsey Island, Wales. More than most birds these auks, living most of the time by swimming and diving, and remaining flightless during their autumn moult of perhaps three weeks at sea, are at risk from the present high oil pollution from tankers. Many thousands are caught in oil slicks and perish miserably: their clogged feathers no longer retain the insulating cushion of warm body air, and some of the poisonous oil is ingested in unsuccessful attempts at preening.

Razorbill, exposed on the ledges of cliffs to the attentions of the large gulls and skuas (which constantly patrol them aerially), need to get their young away as quickly as possible.

It may be asked, why do guillemots (known as murres in America) crowd together almost shoulder to shoulder, and lay their large single egg on narrow ledges on sheer cliffs, in such a dangerous situation? The answer, of course, is quite simple: they do so because those which, down the centuries of their evolution, adapted to such a site have been very successful. So flourishing in fact that until man began to take them, their eggs and chicks for food during the last three centuries of exploiting their remote haunts, the two cliff-breeding guillemots (Common, *Uria aalge*, and Thick-billed, *U. lomvia*) were among the most abundant seabirds in the

world. L.M. Tuck in his book *The Murres* (1960) estimated that about that year there were at least 56 million ledge-nesting murres.

Although gulls, skuas, eagles, falcons and some other aerial enemies seek to snatch egg or chick from the guillemot ledges, normally the adults are so closely ranked that the attack is beaten off by united stabbing of bills, squawking and wing-waving. Those chicks which got away to sea earliest were the ones which survived to carry on the species; and this precocity has resulted today in the young guillemot taking off to sea when less than half-grown, at 18 to 25 days old. It is remarkable to note how they do this, evidently to reduce the chances of attack, late on a July evening when gulls and other predators are usually roosting. For a day or

two previously the chick, its primary flight-feathers not yet developed, patrols the edge of its birthplace, squeaking much and peering down at the sea. One or more adults are meanwhile swimming close by, and answering with a growling note. At last the youngster leaps into space, and manages to flutter downwards, using the stumpy secondary wing-feathers. It may hit a rock, but, fat and cushioned with new feathers, it bounces off safely. Usually two or three adults swim up to the squeaking pioneer excitedly, as if to protect it. Should a predator swoop towards it, all dive – the chick instantly learning the importance of diving and swimming under water to avoid enemies. It does not matter how many adults begin to convoy the youngster away from the danger of the land; when we have subsequently met a juvenile at this stage far at sea, it has had only one adult with it, teaching it how to catch little fishes by diving pursuit under water, and feeding it until it is full-grown and able to fend for itself.

This late parental care contrasts strikingly with the launching of the young Atlantic Puffin. Reared alone in the darkness of a (usually deep) burrow, it has no immediate urge to go to sea. It is fed on raw fish which the parents dump on the earthen floor of the nest-site. This is dry, and absorbs the considerable faecal waste resulting from the bird's diet, but soon, with increasingly large meals, the young bird sets up its own lavatory in a corner of the burrow, as if conscious of the need for hygiene in such a confined situation. It now patters up and down the length of the tunnel but is extremely wary of poking its head outside. Gulls are alert for young Atlantic Puffins daring to do this for the first time, and catch and devour many in large colonies which may number many thousands of pairs. The Puffin chick is now about 35 days old, and its main interest in the outer world is to void its excreta clear of the burrow. This it does, after a cautious peep for enemies, by turning round and squirting it into the open, then hastily scurrying back to dark safety below. About the 40th day the parents are beginning to desert the well-feathered child. It is very fat, and now comes out of the burrow at night to exercise its wings properly for the first time. About the 45th day it no longer returns to the burrow, but walks confidently at night to the sea. Quite alone, it makes its way by swimming – it is not strong on the wing for a while – as fast as possible into the open ocean. It can dive as well as its parents. All the auks swim under water with half-open wings used like paddles, making jerky strokes: the feet help only when moving slowly, otherwise they are trailed behind, like a rudder.

Most of the auks do not breed until they are four to six years old, although they may return home earlier to reconnoitre a future breeding site, arriving a month or two after the mature breeders are in occupation. The more resident species, such as Common, Thick-billed and Black Guillemots, assemble at intervals in large groups below their nesting cliffs and screes, where they indulge in display and simultaneous diving ceremonies, even in midwinter, usually on a fine calm morning. As there is little room to do so on the land at the nesting sites, auks mate on the water, close to their colonies. After completing reproduction, they moult all their flight-feathers at sea within a short period, during which they are unable to fly – nor need to. When they do fly, the effort seems laboursome, a whirring straight-line affair; you have the feeling that they are evolving to become flightless, like the penguins, in a few more thousand years.

The diversity of habitat and behaviour of the group of Pacific auklets is amazing. Four species of murrelets lay two eggs in a burrow, but instead of nursing their chicks in the safety of an underground hole, almost as soon as they hatch their parents chirpingly call them down to the sea at night. The new-born have webbed feet almost as large as those of

Right Common Guillemot or Murre, *Uria aalge*. The single egg is pear-shaped, so does not easily roll, although laid on hard rock. Incubation lasts one month, the chick fledging precociously when only half-grown and then being convoyed away to sea by one adult.

Below A Brünnich's Guillemot or Thick-billed Murre, *U. lomvia*, finds difficulty taking off from a calm sea near the Arctic pack-ice. With their stout bodies and short wings the auks fly whirringly and laboriously in a straight line. But under the water the wings, half-closed, are efficient paddles to propel them rapidly in pursuit of their small fish prey.

The Auks

Below The Atlantic Puffin, *Fratercula arctica*, brings home a beakful of sand eels for its single chick safe within a burrow on the Shetland Isles. Huge colonies breed on many isolated rat-free islands in the North Atlantic, from Spitsbergen south to Britain and the coast of Maine, including Arctic Canada and Greenland. Two allied species nest on the Pacific side: the Horned, *F. corniculata*, and the Tufted, *Lunda cirrhata*.

Right Atlantic Puffins, *Fratercula arctica*, at nesting burrows, taken on Skomer during the evening assembly of these sociable birds.

the adult, an adaptation for instant swimming. When we were in the Bering Sea we observed thousands of Crested Auklets, *Aethia cristatella*, on St Lawrence Island, where they are hunted for food by the island's Eskimo population. In the sea immense flocks were feeding, and there was 'a pleasant smell of tangerines', as my companion in the boat described the aroma. It emanates from the thick, pale-tipped yellow bill; but no one seems to know why this should smell of citrus fruit. Perhaps it has something to do with its diet of euphausid krill which it obtains by diving to the sea floor? We watched these small auks carry this zooplankton in their distended throat-pouches to burrows which they share with lemmings, close under the melting winter snows of that remarkable island, where walruses whelp in early summer. Strange, too, is the habit of the Marbled Murrelet, *Brachyramphus marmoratus*, which flies inland to rear its chick in a hole high up on a forested slope, from British Columbia to Kamchatka; almost nothing is known about its ecology. But perhaps we can close this account of the remarkable lives of the seabirds with a sketch of one of the most bizarre and wonderful in our experience.

The Eskimo Fogbird or Kittlitz's Murrelet, *B. brevirostris*, black and white like the Little Auk of the High (Atlantic) Arctic, and much the same small size, is numerous in the seas between Alaska and Siberia, yet hardly anyone has seen its nesting place. It has lately been found to lay its protectively coloured egg solitarily, in the open, near the summit of ice-cold coastal mountains in Alaska and Siberia, perhaps several kilometres inland. How the lone young fogbird reaches the sea no one has been able to observe. One can only admire how this species must have adapted, under pressure of rival species occupying better situations closer to the sea, to surviving in such a grim habitat by spacing out its nest-sites; by secretive and solitary arrival of the adults, probably at night; and by the lone young bird eventually flying down to the sea (to walk it would risk meeting wolf, fox, falcon, eagle and owl which hunt those solitudes). It is a truly hardy species, haunting the icy waters of glacier-strewn seas.

Saving the Auks

The largest auk of all, standing upright twice as tall as a Razorbill, was flightless. Known as the Great Auk, it was exterminated on the rocky islands and stacks of its Newfoundland, Icelandic and Hebridean haunts by 1844, long hunted by fishermen and native people who found its large body excellent eating. No other seabird has been exterminated within historical times, although the Guadelupe Storm Petrel, *Oceanodroma macrodactyla*, has not been seen since 1911. A few species have become very rare as described earlier in this book. Fortunately today, although many of the auks breeding in Iceland, Greenland, and the Bering Sea area are still taken for food, chiefly as winter provender, measures for their conservation exist by law, and many island sites have been preserved as permanent sanctuaries.

Auks, from living most of their lives swimming in the open sea, are particularly vulnerable to the tarry oil discharged (by design or accident) by tankers, and which floats at the surface, clogging their plumage and destroying the insulation of body heat essential for their survival. Many thousands of auks are washed ashore dead or dying of this lethal black oil every time a large tanker carrying crude oil is wrecked. It is surprising that, after the extensive pollution which then occurs on coasts where auks breed, many have survived. Yet, although many colonies have been decimated

thereby, only one or two of the smallest have been eliminated. (Natural oil, which on some coasts percolates from below the ocean bed in small gaseous emissions into the sea above, actually is believed to have some value – in fat and mineral content – as part of the food chain of the smallest planktonic organisms.) Another threat to the oceanic swimming birds has recently developed in the over-exploitation of their food chain by the increasingly numerous fishing fleets of the world, equipped with highly sophisticated sonar devices and take-all catching nets for finding and harvesting every sort of edible fish, from sharks and tunny to thumbnail-size shrimps. The last – the small crustaceans – are part of the main food of the auks; they are captured by the tonne in close-meshed nets towed behind modern trawlers. While off Spitsbergen in 1982 we watched one of these (Norwegian) trawlers haul a tow-net through its stern slipway (our ship the *Lindblad Explorer* bargained for a few boxes of these shrimps – and very good eating they were, fresh from the ocean). But earlier, visiting some of the small islands off Norway famous for their huge Atlantic Puffin colonies, we were sad to find that very few adults were carrying food; there was not enough to feed both themselves and their single chick. Most of these were dead in the burrows, or thin and emaciated; and some eggs had not even been hatched.

A similar shortage of the shrimp, sardine, capelin and anchoveta food of seabirds elsewhere in the world's temperate seas, due to overfishing by man, has had the same

Right Despite their precarious nesting place on narrow cliff ledges the guillemots or murres have been highly successful up to the present time, evolving a defence against aerial predators (gulls, skuas) by crowding together in tight rows and lunging with their sharp pointed bills.

Left Close-up of the head of *Alca torda*, the Razorbill, showing its structural resemblance to that of the Great Auk. In this breeding dress the mouth is kept open for long periods, to display the pale yellow interior. The compressed hooked bill is able to catch and hold several small fish at the same time, when returning from sea to feed the single chick in some sheltered crevice in steep cliffs. Inhabits low Arctic and temperate coasts both sides of the Atlantic.

inhibiting effect on their breeding success. But overfishing has brought other disasters – for the fishermen; there has been overproduction, resulting in fierce competition for world markets, and uneconomic prices which no longer make it worth operating expensive fishing vessels. When we visited the Westmann Islands, south of Iceland, a centre for the cod and capelin fisheries, we found that the capelin, main food of the puffins and other auks, had 'failed' in that season of 1982. That is to say, catches were no longer large enough and the price per tonne was so low, that trying to fish for them was no longer worthwhile. Westmann islanders depend entirely on fish for a living. They also traditionally take a moderate number of seabirds to cure for winter eating. But they are a compassionate community; and one of the annual conservation tasks is to collect the many young Atlantic Puffins which, leaving their burrows for the sea at night, in August, are found wandering through the little seaport next morning. They are kept safely over the day, to be released in the sea the next evening, when the predatory gulls and skuas are roosting.

Seabirds can survive and even increase if they have enough food and their natural homes are protected, even in a busy shipping area like the North Sea which today also has numerous drilling platforms producing petroleum oil. On the bird reserves of the Farne Isles off Northumberland, and at the Isle of May in the Firth of Forth, there has been a considerable increase in the protected puffin population during this present period of oil-drilling development.

A final cheerful note. Conservationists in the United States conceived the idea of attempting to restore to Eastern Egg Rock, Maine, its former large colony of Atlantic Puffins. This had been exterminated in the last century by fishermen who netted the seabirds for use as bait in their lobster traps, and earlier as food and for their feathers (for the millinery trade). With support from the National Audubon Society, volunteers collected young puffins from Newfoundland's abundant puffinries, transferred them to artificial burrows on Egg Rock, fed them, and eventually allowed them to go to sea naturally. They correctly premised that, when ready to begin breeding, these youngsters would return to the only place they knew as home. It meant that the experiment would have to be repeated each summer, in order to establish a succession of new colonists of maturing age-groups. The first batch was introduced in 1973. To encourage these sociable birds to land in the right place when they did first return, life-sized painted decoys were planted in life-like attitudes on the rock. Of the 530 transplanted puffins old enough to have returned by 1981, 111 (or 21 percent) have been sighted – wearing an identification band. The puffins are now breeding naturally again at Eastern Egg Rock, Maine. 'Truly a triumph – to re-establish puffins to a former breeding site', comments S.W. Kress (1982), 'but to secure the puffins' future, we need a world-wide commitment to work towards maintaining the highest possible productivity and diversity of the seas.'

Left Common Guillemot, *Uria aalge*, killed by oil.

Right In June 1844 the last Great Auk, *Alca impennis*, a giant flightless Razorbill, was exterminated on the rock stack of Eldey, south of Iceland. This photograph was taken in the Museum at Reykjavik, the capital. In the previous century its main known haunt was Funk Island off the Newfoundland coast, where visiting European fishermen for two centuries had provisioned their boats in summer by driving these hapless 'penguins', as they were called, on board over sails laid between ship and shore, before salting them down.

Index

Aethia cristatella 153
Albatross: Black-browed *see Diomedia melanophris*; Black-footed *see D. nigripes*; Buller's *see D. bulleri*; Grey-headed *see D. chrysostoma*; Laysan *see D. immutabilis*; Light-mantled Sooty *see Phoebetria palpebrata*; Royal *see Diomedea epomophora*; Short-tailed *see D. albatrus*; Wandering *see D. exulans*; Waved *see D. irrorata*; White-capped or Shy *see D. cauta*; Yellow-nosed *see D. chlororhynchos*
Albatrosses 66–73
Alca: impennis 154, *157*; *torda* 147, *148, 148–9*, 154, *154*
Alexander, W. B. 10–11
Alle alle 147, 153
Anhinga melanogaster 103
Anous: stolidus 20–1; *tenuirostris* 144
Aptenodytes: forsteri 54, 60–4; *patagonicus* 50, 60–1, *62–3, 64–5*
Apus apus 136
Auckland Isles 56, 68, 106
Auk: Great *see Alca impennis*; Little *see Alle alle*
Auklet, Crested *see Aethia cristatella*
Auks 154

Bass Strait 89
Bear Island 121
Bermuda 87
Benguela current 55, 138
Bergmann's Rule 54
Booby: Blue-footed *see Sula nebouxii*; Masked or Blue-faced *see S. dactylatra*; Red-footed *see S. sula*
Bos'n birds *see tropicbirds*
Bounty Island 104
Brachyramphus: brevirostris 153; *marmoratus* 153

Cahow *see Pterodroma cahow*
Calonectris diomedea 84, 85

Campbell Islands 68, 106
Catharacta: maccormicki 120–1, 121, 122–3, 136; *skua* 120, 121, 122–3, 124
Cepphus grylle 146–7, 147, 150
Chatham Islands 88–9, 104
Chionis alba 48–9
Chlidonias: hybridus 143; *leucopterus* 143; *niger* 28
Christmas Island 110
Cormorant: Blue-eyed or Antarctic *see Phalacrocorax atriceps*; Brandt's *see P. penicillatus*; Campbell Island *see P. campbElli*; European *see P. carbo*; Galapagos or Flightless *see Nannopterum harrisi*; King *see Phalacrocorax albiventor*; Little Black *see P. sulcirostris*; Pelagic *see P. pelagicus*; Pied *see P. varius*; Reed *see Halietor africanus*; White-necked *see Phalacrocorax lucidus*
Cormorants and shags 100, 104–8
Creagrus furcatus 20, 135, *137*

Daption capense 78–9, *82–3*
Darter, African *see Anhinga melanogaster*
Darters 13, 100
Diomedea: albatrus 60; *bulleri* 68, 77, 78–9; *cauta* 68, 74–5; *chlororhynchos* 68; *chrysostoma* 68; *epomophora* 58, 66, 68; *exulans* 67, 68, 69; *immutabilis* 66; *irrorata* 55, 67, 68, 70–1; *melanophris* 68, 72, 73, 75, 76–7; *nigripes* 66
Diving petrels 94
Drake, Francis 55

Eastern Egg Rock 156
El Nino 55
Enderby Island 56
Eudyptes: chrysocome 44–5, 47, 58, 58; *chrysolophus* 58, 58; *pachyrhynchus* 58; *robustus* 58; *schlegeli* 50, 58, 58; *sclateri* 58

Eudyptula minor 50–1, 53, 54, 55–6, 58
Evolution 44–7

Faeroe Islands 93
Falkland Islands 55, 60, 79
Farne Isles 156
Fisher Island 99
Fogbird, Eskimo *see Brachyramphus bravirostris*
Fratercula arctica 147, 150, *152–3, 153*, 154, 156
Fregata: magnificens 96, 98; *minor* 97
Frigatebird: Great *see Fregata minor*; Magnificent *see F. magnificens*
Frigatebirds or man-of-war birds 96–8, 102, 106, 110, 125
Fulmar: Northern *see Fulmarus glacialis*; Southern *see F. glacialoides*
Fulmarus: glacialis 75–6, 80, *80–1*; *glacialoides* 75, 78
Fulmars 73–7, *78–9*

Gabianus scoresbyi 28–9
Galapagos Islands 13, 55, 67, 135
Gannet: Australasian *see Sula serrator*; Cape or South African *see S. capensis*; North Atlantic *see S. bassana*
Gannets and boobies 100–4, 106
Gelochelidon nilotica 142
Giant Petrel: Northern *see Macronectes halli*; Southern *see M. giganteus*
Giant petrels 68, 73–5, 79
Grassholm 104
Guillemot: Black *see Cepphus grylle*; Brünnich's or Thick-billed *see Uria lomvia*; Common *see U. aalge*
Guillemots (Murres) 146, 147–50
Gull: Bonaparte's *see Larus philadelphia*; Californian *see L. californicus*; Common or Mew *see L. canus*; Dolphin or Magellan *see Gabianus scoresbyi*; Dominican or Kelp *see Larus dominicanus*; European Black-headed *see L. ridibundus*; Glaucous *see L. hyperboreus*; Glaucous-winged *see L. glaucescens*; Great Black-backed *see L. marinus*; Great Black-headed *see L. ichthyaetus*; Heermann's *see L. Heermanni*; Herring *see L. argentatus*; Indian Brown-headed *see L. brunnicephalus*; Ivory *see Pagophila eburnea*; Laughing *see Larus atricilla*; Lave or Dusky *see L. fuliginosus*; Lesser Black-backed *see L. fuscus*; Little *see L. minutus*; Pacific *see L. pacificus*; Ring-billed *see L. delawarensis*; Sabine's *see L. sabini*; Silver *see L. novaehollandiae*; Sooty or Aden *see L. hemprichi*; Swallow-tailed *see Creagrus furcatus*; Western *see Larus occidentalis*

Gulls 125–35
Gygis alba 125, *140–1, 142, 142*, 145

Halobaena caerulea 80, 87
Halietor africanus 108
Hauaraki Gulf 124
Hearing 23
Hen, Cape *see Procellaria aequinoctialis*
Hood Island 67
Humboldt current 55, 67, 94, 118, 138
Hydrobates pelagicus 10, 93, 94

Isle of May 10, 156

Jaeger; Arctic *see Stercorarius parasiticus*; Long-tailed *see S. longicaudus*
Jaegers 120, 124, 125
Jan Mayen 75

Kittiwake: (Black-legged) *see Rissa tridactyla*; Red-legged *see R. brevirostris*

Larosterna inca 36–7
Larus: argentatus 10–11, 129, *129*, 133–5; *atricilla* 133; *brunnicephalus* 128; *californicus* 128; *canus* 132; *delawarensis* 133; *dominicanus* 122–3, 130, *130–1*, 135; *fuliginosus* 135, 137; *fuscus* 16–17, 129, 135; *glaucescens* 135; *heermanni* 26; *hemprichi* 136; *hyperboreus* 8–9, 129, 131, 134, 135; *ichthaetus* 136; *marinus* 129, *131*, 135; *minutus* 137; *novaehollandiae* 18–19, 130, 131, 135; *occidentalis* 135, *135*; *pacificus* 30–1, 135; *philadelphia* 38–9; *ridibundus* 132, *133*; *sabini* 27
Las Platas Island 67
Linnaeus 100

Macquarie Island 50, 58, 60, 73, 106
Macronectes: giganteus 73; *halli* 74
Marlinspike, *see tropicbirds*
Mawson, Sir Douglas 50
Megadyptes antipodes 56–8, 59
Mollymawks 68–73
Murphy, Robert Cushman 64
Murrelet: Kittlitz's *see Brachyramphus brevirostris*; Marbled *see B. marmoratus*
Murrelets 150–3

Nannopterum harrisi 14, 55, 104, *104*
Noddies 125, 142
Noddy: Common or Brown *see Anous stolidus*; Lesser *see A. tenuirostris*
Norfolk Island 145

Oceanites oceanicus 93, *93*
Oceanodroma: castro 84–5; *leucorhoa* 88; *macrodactyla* 154
Outer Hebrides 76

Pachyptila turtur 84–5
Pagodroma nivea 80–1, 86
Pagophila eburnea 134
Pelagodroma marina 84, 85
Penguin: Adelie *see Pygoscelis adeliae*; Chinstrap *see P. antarctica*; Emperor *see Aptenodytes forsteri*; Erect-crested *see Eudyptes sclateri*; Fiordland *see E. pachyrhynchus*; Galapagos *see Spheniscus mendiculus*; Gentoo *see Pygoscelis papua*; Jackass, Blackfoot or Cape *see Spheniscus demersus*; King *see Aptenodytes patagonicus*; Little Blue or Fairy *see Eudyptula minor*; Macaroni *see Eudyptes chrysolophus*; Magellan *see Spheniscus magellanicus*; Peruvian *see S. humboldti*; Rockhopper *see Eudyptes chrysocome*; Royal *see E. schlegeli*; Snares Island *see E. robustus*; Yellow-eyed *see Megadyptes antipodes*
Penguins 47–65
Petrel: Antarctic *see Thalassoica antarctica*; Black *see Procellaria parkinsoni*; Blue *see Halobaena caerulea*; British Storm *see Hydrobates pelagicus*; Cape *see Daption capense*; Frigate or White-faced *see Pelagodroma marina*; Great-winged or Grey-faced *see Pterodroma macroptera*; Guadalupe *see Oceanodroma macrodactyla*; Leach's *see O. leucorhoa*; Madeiran *see O. castro*; Silver-grey *see Fulmarus glacialoides*; Snow *see Pagodroma nivea*; Westland Black *see Procellaria westlandica*; White-chinned *see P. aequinoctialis*; Wilson's Storm *see Oceanites oceanicus*
Phaethon: aethereus 108, 116–17; lepturus 108, 110, 116; rubricauda 108, 110
Phaetusa simplex 22
Phalacrocorax: albiventer 109; aristotelis 115; atriceps 104, 105; campbelli 111; carbo 14, 115; carunculatus 110–11; lucidus 12–13, 112–13; melanoleucus 24–5; pelagicus 14–15, 108–9; penicillatus 14–15; punctatus 71; sulcirostris 34–5; varius 106–8, 106–7
Phalarope: Grey *see Phalaropus fulicarius*; Red-necked *see P. lobatus*; Wilson's *see P. tricolor*
Phalaropes 13, 117–18
Phalaropus: fulicarius 117, 118–19; lobatus 117, 118–19; tricolor 117
Phillip Island 56
Phoebetria palpebrata 72–3, 73
Pigeon, Cape *see Daption capense*
Pintado *see Daption capense*
Pitt Island 104
Prion, Fairy *see Pachyptila turtur*
Prions 78, 79–80

Procellaria: aequinoctialis 88; parkinsoni 87; westlandica 87
Pterodroma: cahow 87–8; macroptera 85, 87; magentae 88–9
Puffin, Atlantic *see Fratercula arctica*
Puffinus: assimilis 84, 85; gavia 89; gravis 85; griseus 94–5; huttoni 89; lherminieri 87, 88–9; pacificus 90–1; puffinus 10, 89, 92–3; tenuirostris 56, 92
Pygoscelis: adeliae 48–9, 53, 58–60; antarctica 60, 60–1; papua 46–7, 50, 60, 64

Razorbill *see Alca torda*
Rissa: brevirostris 125–6; tridactyla 125–8, 126–7
Rockall 85
Ross Island 58, 63, 122

St Lawrence Island 153
Seaward Kaikoura Mountains 89
Selvagen Islands 84–5
Serventy, Dom 89, 92
Shag: European *see Phalacrocorax aristotelis*; Little *see P. melanoleucus*; Spotted *see P. punctatus*; Stewart Island *see P. carunculatus*
Shearwater: Audubon's *see Puffinus lherminieri*; Cory's *see Calonectris diomedea*; Fluttering *see Puffinus gavia*; Great *see P. gravis*; Hutton's *see P. huttoni*; Little *see P. assimilis*; Manx *see P. puffinus*; Short-tailed *see P. tenuirostris*; Sooty *see P. griseus*; Wedge-tailed *see P. pacificus*
Shearwaters 81–92
Sheathbill, Yellow-billed *see Chionis alba*
Sheathbills 114–17
Shetland Islands 73, 124
Shoemaker *see Procellaria aequinoctialis*
Skimmers 145
Skokholm 8, 10, 89, 93
Skua: Arctic *see Stercorarius parasiticus*; Great *see Catharacta skua*; Long-tailed *see Stercorarius longicaudus*; South Polar *see Catharacta maccormicki*
Skuas and Jaegers 120–4, 125
Smell 23
Sooty albatrosses 68
South Georgia Island 60, 64, 79, 104
South Sandwich Islands 60
Spheniscus: demersus 55, 56–7; humboldti 53, 55; magellanicus 53, 54–5, 55; mendiculus 52, 54, 55
Spitsbergen 75, 136, 154
Stercorarius: longicaudus 123; parasiticus 40–1, 124, 124–5, 136
Sterna: albifrons 27; anaethetus 19; bengalensis 145; caspia 138, 138–9; dougallii 23; fuscata 32–3, 125, 136, 138–42; hirundo 138,

144; paradisaea 18, 136, 138, 145; sandvicensis 138, 145; striata 139; vittata 136, 138
Stonehouse, Bernard 53
Storm petrels 93
Sula: bassana 73, 98–9, 100, 102, 104; capensis 104; dactylatra 101; nebouxii 100; serrator 104; sula 102
Swift, European *see Apus apus*

Taiaroa Head 68
Taiko *see Pterodroma magentae*
Taste, 23
Tern: Antarctic *see Sterna vittata*; Arctic *see S. paradisaea*; Black *see Chlidonias niger*; Bridled or Brown-winged *see Sterna anaethetus*; Caspian *see S. caspia*; Common *see S. hirundo*; Elegant *see Thalasseus elegans*; Gull-billed *see Gelochelidon nilotica*; Inca *see Larosterna inca*; Large-billed *see Phaetusa simplex*; Lesser Crested *see Sterna bengalensis*; Little *see S. albifrons*; Roseate *see S. dougallii*; Sandwich *see S. sandvicensis*; Sooty *see S. fuscata*; Whiskered *see Chlidonias hybridus*; White *see Gygis alba*; White-fronted *see Sterna striata*; White-fronted Black *see Chlidonias leucopterus*
Terns 136–45
Thalasseus elegans 42–3
Thalassoica antarctica 81, 86–7
Tierra del Fuego 55
Toroshima 67
Tristan da Cunha 85
Tropicbird: Red-billed *see Phaeton aethereus*; Red-tailed *see P. rubricauda*; White-tailed *see P. lepturus*
Tropicbirds 108–10

Uria: aalge 148, 148–9, 150, 151, 155, 156; lomvia 148, 150, 150–1

Vision 20

Water needs 23
Westmann Islands 156
Whalebirds 78
Wilson, Edward 61
Whitherby, Harry F. 10

Young, E. C. 122

Zavodovski Island 60

Note: page numbers in italics denote illustrations.

Bibliography

Diamond, A. W. (1972) *Ibis* 114: 395
Fisher, J. & R. M. Lockley (1964) Seabirds of the North Atlantic
Harris, M. (1970) *Auk* 87: 215–24
—— (1974) Field Guide to Birds of Galapagos
Harrison, R. J. and G. L. Kooyman (1971) *Diving in Marine Mammals*, Oxford University Press
Imber, M. J. (1976) *Ibis* 118: 51–64
Kress, S. W. (1982) *The Living Bird Quarterly* 1: 11–14 (Lab. Orn. Cornell University)
Matthews, L. H. (1929) Birds of South Georgia (*Discovery Reports* 1: 561–92)
Mills, J. A. (1973) *Journ. Animal Ecology* 42: 147–62
Nelson, B. (1968) Galapagos
—— (1978) The Gannet
—— (1980) Seabirds: their Biology and Ecology
Richdale, C. E. (1939–64) Numerous publications on petrels breeding in New Zealand
Salomonsen, F. (1976) *Dansk. Orn. Foren Tidssk.*: 70: 81–9
Serventy, D. (1963) *Proceedings XIII Orn. Congress* 1: 338–43
Stonehouse, B. (ed.) (1975) The Biology of Penguins
Tasker, C. R. & J. A. Mills (1981) *Behaviour* 77: 4, 221–41
Young, E. C. (1972) *Ibis*: 234–44